Heritage Edition

This Book Belongs to:

Write your name here after the previous owner when you inherit this book!

By the time you finish reading this book you will realise the importance of something passing down nine generations!

If you are giving this book **to your own child**, write your name first and then write their name after yours!

Start this legacy now!

Name   Date

Harrison of The North of Branthwaite

Name   Date

The Secret Cypher of Edward The Confessor

Decyphering Edward the Confessor's Deathbed Dream of 1066

- First Edition -

Anthony Harrison
'Harrison of The North of Branthwaite'

- A Raven Lore Children's Series -

Harrison of The North of Branthwaite

Published by the Habspruch Press

for Habspruch Abbey

Cumberland, Great Britain
publisher@habspruch.com

Copyright © Harrison of The North of Branthwaite 2024

1. **Reading Audience**: For Advanced Learners with a "Flesch Reading Ease" Score of 50 or less (Chapter Average).
2. **Reading Suitability**: The book is suitable for readers who are comfortable with more complex texts, such as aged 10+ who are advanced readers, high school seniors, college students, adults who read regularly.
3. **Language Style**: The writing style includes a variety of sentence structures and a moderate use of more advanced vocabulary. It's not overly simplistic, but it's also not highly technical or academic.
4. **Comprehension**: Readers might need to pay attention and possibly reread some sections to fully grasp the material, especially where it includes abstract concepts or specialized terms.
5. **Rule of Thumb**: A Flesch Reading Ease Score of 65 is about the same level as Reader's Digest magazine.

Quotes

"In the Dream, two Benedictine Monks whom Edward had previously known in Normandy, came to him and pronounced that 'because of England's great sins, a great tree would be cut down, and at a distance of three furlongs, green branches would reattach themselves to the roots of the tree and flourish by their own accord'."

Edward the Confessor's Deathbed Dream, 1066, Paraphrased by The Author

"The farther backward you can look, the farther forward you are likely to see."

Winston Churchill

"This book covers 12,500 years of The Ascent of Arthurian Britain"

Harrison of The North of Branthwaite—The Author

"Edward the Confessor was seen as the quintessential Christian king, whose reign was a moral and spiritual beacon in the history of the English monarchy."

Simon Schama, in his book "A History of Britain"

The spelling of the word "**forest**" as "**forrest**" is intentional in this book.

It is an ellipse to "**The Great Arthurian Oaken Forrest**".

By the end of this book, you will discover that the oaken trees of The Great Arthurian Oaken Forrest are *foremost*, giving The Great Arthurian Oaken Forrest **pre-eminence** over all forests.

This relates to the Awen of "The Battle of The Trees".

Dedication

To those who wish to hold the truth within their hearts—and to those who will learn it anyway!

Presenting the past, present, and future of Britain in remembrance of **The Four Great Prophecies of Arthurian Britain**:

1. So long as the Head of Bran faces south on Britain's White Mount, Britain will be protected. 1st Century. (n.b. "Bran" means raven.)
2. Arthur will return as a raven. Post-'Age of Arthur'. (n.b. "arth" means bear.)
3. The Red Dragon will be temporarily wounded by The White Dragon, but then The Red Dragon will rise and kill The White Dragon. Post-'Age of Arthur'.
4. So long as there are ravens in the Tower of London, England will be protected. Post-1066, an evolution of the previous 1st-century Prophecy of Bran.

All of British History should be interpreted with respect to these Four Great Prophecies of Arthurian Britain—accordingly, the Prophecy of Edward the Confessor's Deathbed Dream of the Year 1066 is interpreted herein in the context of these four great prophecies!

Harrison of The North of Branthwaite

Preface

Children are well aware that if they wake up first, their whole house wakes up with them; there is little that can suppress the love and joy of a beloved child!

This, in part, is one reason why I write books for children: in many families, it is the awakening child who wakes the adult. So, for that reason, I write about Arthurian history, realising that where children awaken to its vigour, many adults will as well—if even just for the reason that children grow into adults!

As an author, I often think that the winning of a Nobel Prize in Literature would be one thing, but *the reason* that one would win a Nobel Prize in Literature would be distinctly another—and the better.

In appealing to the child in you, please consider which of these would be more important.

Is it more important that **someone is named** as having won a Nobel Prize in Literature, or that **the reason why they won it** is named?

Nobel Prizes in Literature are usually listed *by Year* and *Author Name*—not by *The Reason* the judges awarded them that lofty accolade in the first place!

Yet, what does the name *Sir Vidiadhar Surajprasad Naipaul* mean to the ordinary person?

Those of us who hold him to be a literary hero of our time could quite easily host a dinner party that celebrates his name—yet to those who have never heard of him, his name is more a challenge to pronounce than something to celebrate.

- Settle on saying **Sir Vid-EE-ar Nye-Paul** to get past this hurdle!

His Year of 2001 was a very good year for those still celebrating that The Millennium Bug did not ruin the world, who in the early stages of 2001 were not yet transfixed on the later tragedy of the destruction of The World Trade Centre.

Ironically, the 24/7 broadcast of 9/11 suppressed what could have heralded a decade of retrospection and then another decade of revolution.

It didn't help that the Nobel Committee itself can turn any wonderfully colourful topic into a description that is beige at best—but to every ethnic minority worldwide, Sir Vidiadhar's 10/11 prize was a beacon of light in the night:

- "for having united perceptive narrative and incorruptible scrutiny in works that compel us to see the presence of **suppressed** histories"

Perhaps it would be better that the recipients wrote these statements, themselves!

Minorities are typically well versed in this topic, and it can typically be summarised in the equally beige statement:

- "The 'Plurality of Multiculturalism' is *most* effective at **marginalising**, **suppressing**, and **obfuscating** the individual minorities that it was originally set up to protect!"

Of course, the problem with this statement is that it is just as beige as the reason the Nobel Committee gave for Sir Vidiadhar's winning this most prestigious prize in Literature in the first place.

It's not until you read Naipaul's breakthrough novel *A House for Mr Biswas*, published in 1961, that you realise how graphic and colourful the pedestal is that Sir Vidiadhar now stands on.

Naturally, Sir Vidiadhar worked to "unite perceptive narrative and in-corruptible scrutiny" on the sup-pressed *Trinidadian and Indian herit-ages* of his own background—but in having done so, he showed everyone else how to do it.

Yet it wasn't this that gave Sir Vidi-adhar his superhero status!

When the Nobel Prize in Literature is awarded, the Nobel Prize Committee causes the whole world to sit still for a moment and consider that "this" is important: in Sir Vidiadhar's case, the 'this' was the revelation that it was important **to restore margin-alised**, **suppressed**, **and obfuscated heritages to public visibility**.

Naturally, I've broadened the tau-tologies of the word 'suppressed' to include 'marginalised' and 'obfuscated', which in doing so qualifies the original abstraction with being connected to those quantifiable processes which caused it to be suppressed.

Where beige transposes to one's enriched vivid experience of it—and this, in Sir Vidiadhar's case, would be acquired by exposing one's emotions to Naipaul's dramatic visualisations of "Mr Biswas's circumstance in the setting of his house"—the lesson that his work extrudes is that "one's success is inevitably tied to one's capability in getting the world to draw its spotlight around to the new focus of dwelling on the particular suppressed heritage that one wants to restore to public visibility".

In my own case, I'm an *Arthurian addict*. I focus on the implications that our Arthurian **past** already has on both our **present** and our **future**.

Naturally, I have to apologise for the use of the word 'addict'—and that's because of its frequent attachment to *dependencies* that are typically ill-thought of.

Yet, if you look at the etymology of the word 'addict', it is very revealing:

- **Addict:** Borrowed from Latin *ad-dictus*—perfect passive participle of *addico* ("assign, hand over")—past participle of *addico* ("deliver; devote; surrender"), from *ad-* ("to, towards, at") + *dico* ("say; declare")

The News Flash here is that, by definition, every person has already surrendered to their past—one's ethnic past is the dependency that one's ethnic present and ethnic future relies upon.

There can be no present or future without their inherent dependency on both having a past.

- Therefore, if one wants one's ethnic present and ethnic future to be preserved, then one must be an addict of one's ethnic past!

Even to the layman, the word addict breaks down to *ad* ('to or towards') the *dict* ('diction of what we say')— and how this relates to the subject of one's ethnic future having a dependency on the history of one's ethnic past, its sum is illustrated in my case where always being *an Arthurian addict in the present* is an accolade.

Although I won't dwell on it any further here, I regard my ethnicity as being an *Orthodox Celt*—a Briton one at that!

Indeed, I see no difference between an Orthodox Jew or a Muslim rightly being recognised under their respective ethnic names, as I similarly also exercise such a right and thus should also be recognised as an Orthodox Celt under the precepts of the same prerogative that afforded those others their rightful distinctions!

Where 'the beige' of this subject turns into the vivid colours of our ethnic experience is that in Britain, our Celtic ancestors developed a compact method of transporting our ethnic heritage *from the past, through the present, into the future*—it is called "Awen"; although it can be described in clinical terms as merely being a *muse*, it can better be defined using an Expression of Awen itself by saying that:

- **Awen** can be described as "a poetic breeze of inspiration that causes meanings to rise as if they were 'eagles of evangelism' soaring on a rising breeze".

This is meant in the sense that these poetic 'eagles of evangelism' fly so high as being imbued with truths that would otherwise be quite complex to say yet are simultaneously distributed as though the wider meaning is conveyed 'evangelically'; that is, the broader complex meaning is conveyed 'on the wings of the eagles'.

Although this topic is expanded over the full course of this book, I'll illustrate it by saying that Arthurian folklore is filled with Secret Cyphers that can be expanded to explain broader truths.

For example, you may have heard about 'The Lady of The Lake', who is core to the Arthurian adventure—yet would you be surprised to learn that "The Secret Cypher of The Lady of The Lake" breaks into two more Secret Cyphers, The Secret Cypher of The Lady, and The Secret Cypher of The Lake—and even these reveal an additional one, the Secret Cypher *of the Relationship between* The Lady *and* The Lake—which, as it turns out, is the Secret Cypher of Evangelism!

With all of this in mind, as an author who is also a businessman, I've had to stand back and wonder about what "the business is" that, as an author, I'm already in.

Putting beige back on the pedestal, I've decided that my Mission Statement is as follows—and as you will plainly see, I have to thank Sir Vidiadhar Naipaul for its broad scope:

Mission Statement: To raise the profile of the **marginalised**, the **suppressed**, and the **obfuscated** heritage of Indigenous Britons and native Britain, using:

• Print and Digital Publishing,
• Multimedia Presentations,
• Public and Guest Speaking,
• Mentorship and Advocacy,
• Lobbying and Activism, and
• Community and Political Leadership.

Naturally, I encourage others who are inspired to draw the quill to consider a similar Mission Statement, but one that represents the particular heritage that they would want to be drawn back into the visibility of the public eye.

And for those who also have Arthurian interests, I encourage you to join me around this literary round table, not only is there seating enough for all of us, there are more than 40 million of us in Britain who might be described as 'ravens who are asleep in our nests' but who will have voracious appetites when awakened. Worldwide, this number must be in the hundreds of millions.

How all of this relates to the readership of this book—broadly, *Children who are Advanced Learners*, as well as *Adults who want to read about our heritage without being exposed to its politics*—is that the Heritage of Britain is really a treasure chest of Secret Cyphers waiting to be rediscovered!

- Who would have thought that "The

Ascent of Arthurian Britain" could be proven to cover as wide a range as 12,500 years—from the melt of the last Ice Age to the present?

- How can Britain's past, present, and future be entirely encapsulated by The Four Great Prophecies of Arthurian Britain?

These two questions are the headwaters of the 'Great Arthurian River'—our 'silvern ribbon' that flows from 'The South' to 'The North'?

To immerse ourselves a little deeper in this subject, we should be asking ourselves "How can Christians, Jews, and Muslims interpret the Arthurian prophecy 'Arthur will return as a raven' in a context that respects their individual faiths?"

Fortunately, Edward the Confessor—one of England's most famous ancient kings—had a monumentally prophetic deathbed dream in the Year of his death, 1066.

Significantly, Edward the Confessor was the only king of England to have been made a saint by both the Roman Catholic Church and the Church of England, and he having been a king as well as a saint of the church, propels the interpretation of the dream directly into the realms of *both* Church *and* State in Britain!

Naturally, it is because this topic is expressed by British citizens who are also members of the Church of England's *congregation*, that the leaders of both Church and State are compelled to subject it to the *already established* formal mechanics of the due processes of both.

The curious thing about this is not just that the deathbed dream was considered to be prophetic by both of these churches—and indeed, the Archbishop of Canterbury, then a member of both The Roman Catholic Church and the Church of England, was actually present when Edward originally told his close-circle about the dream—and here, the curious context of the symbols that were projected by the dream can be seen to interleave directly with some of the most significant of Arthurian imagery of all time!

This means that the process of properly interpreting the dream also requires the process of properly resolving many of its interleaving Arthurian Secret Cyphers—hence, these also need to be subject to the *already established* proper mechanics of the due processes of both The Church and The State in Britain!

In this book, *The Secret Cypher of Edward the Confessor,* I present an interpretation of Edward the Confessor's Deathbed Dream that treats every component of it as a range of Secret Cyphers that each need to be afforded their own due attention by those already established mechanics of formal due process that both

Church and State legally require.

On the one hand, the State would seem to be predisposed **to fear** that any interpretation of Edward the Confessor's Deathbed Dream would be subject to the already established due processes of 'the Ecclesiastical People'.

This is because the following of Nostradamus's prophecies seems to put the prospect of "the ecclesiastical people's" *judgement* as having an *adverse* effect upon the State:

Century 1, Quatrain 49, by Nostradamus

The river that tries the new Celtic heir
Will be in great discord with the Empire:
The young Prince through the ecclesiastical people
Will remove the sceptre of the crown of concord.

On the other hand, the State's fear of the Church is exemplified in the matter that the same prophecy implies that the Church will not deviate from expressing The Truth in the matter under discussion.

Also, it's probably worthwhile quoting the proverb: "As iron sharpens iron, so one person sharpens another." (NIV).

As much as the institutionalised Church of England might tend to gravitate towards preserving the interests of The British State, the other ecclesiastic player in this circumstance is the Roman Catholic Church—which doesn't seem to have a vested interest in the matters of 'The State' in this modern day—and yet, the Roman Catholic Church was originally present around Edward the Confessor's Deathbed in the person of the then *Roman Catholic* Archbishop of Canterbury ~ *its recognised historical witness!*

In this sense, the above proverb can be written as a contrafactum that exudes a similar truth:

- "As iron sharpens iron, so the Roman Catholic Church sharpens the Church of England."

Naturally, this can also be expressed as the conjugate:

- "As iron sharpens iron, so the Church of England sharpens the Roman Catholic Church."

However in this circumstance, no matter how the Church of England might be tempted to not deviate from the interests of The British State, it is quite clear that the Roman Catholic Church is 'The Gatekeeper' that is intended to keep 'the ecclesiastical people' of the Church of England on their proper bearing.

Let's not forget that these issues are relevant to the individual personages of every Christian in Britain, and to the individual personages of every Christian worldwide who has British interests.

Profoundly, these issues are just as relevant to every Jew and Muslim in Britain as well—and also to every Jew and Muslim worldwide who has British interests—and this is because (as explained in my book *The Secret Cypher of Chalice Well*), the 'Arthurian Cycle of Britain' is equally relevant to every Jew and Muslim in Britain, who in the context of 'The Arthurian Dream' are on the very same footing as every Christian in Britain.

- To illustrate this with a minor example, I'd think that every Jew or Muslim has the very same reason to climb Glastonbury Tor and look into the rising sun on the morning of the Summer Solstice, as Christians would find reason to do so: the "Secrets of Chalice Well" are open to all faiths, as are the rewards of "finding the Holy Grail". (You should refer to my book above for more information on this topic.)

Naturally, this prospect broadens the

role of the Roman Catholic Church to the sceptre of representing the interests of all three 'tribes of Abraham' in this matter—the tribe of Christians, the tribe of Jews, and the tribe of Muslims.

As Gatekeeper, it is the role of the Roman Catholic Church to ensure that no aspect of a full and proper interpretation of Edward the Confessor's Deathbed Dream is **marginalised, suppressed,** or **obfuscated**.

Here, even the Roman Catholic Church is surrounded by additional stalwarts of the truth in support of its gate-keeping role: not only does this include the Christian, Jewish, and Muslim communities at large, but it also includes such highly esteemed proponents of truth as the Nobel Prize Committee itself.

- Yet how relevant is this particular 'Prophecy of Nostradamus' to the modern day?

Just to be pragmatic, this quatrain has been widely believed for many years to relate to the era starting around 2023 and 2024—in this sense, this topic is already being propelled by pre-existing public perception!

Yet no matter how things unfold, we are in effect protected by "Excalibur"—the 'double-edged Sword of Truth' that was wielded by Arthur and returned to The Lady of The Lake when Arthur died—here, you can take "The Lady" to represent 'The Church', as explained in my first book in this series, *The Secret Cypher of Chalice Well*—so, the wonderful thing about the nature of all of these Secret Cyphers is that not only were they originally created so that they could just as well be understood by children as by adults, but their truth is plain for everyone to see, whether seen by children or seen by adults!

This book is number 2 of a series of three books that I'm publishing on

Arthurian Secret Cyphers:

1. **The Secret Cypher of Chalice Well.** This introduces the nature of hundreds of Arthurian Secret Cyphers, illustrating how they are just as relevant to Muslims and Jews, as they are to Christians and other faiths.

2. **The Secret Cypher of Edward the Confessor.** This introduces how the Arthurian past, present, and future, of Britain, were originally predestined to be interleaved with Church and State.

3. **The Secret Cypher of Why There Are Ravens in the Tower of London.** This identifies a looming epoch that is necessary for "Arthur to return as a raven" at some future point in time.

To all of you who identify as 'Cyphers' of this openly secret club, I wish you Godspeed—Tally-Ho, good and faithful steed!

- The Author, Cumberland, Great Britain

Contents

What do you think that the Secret Cypher of this image means?

This image represents the **Crux of Arthurian Canon**, *the prophecy "Arthur will return as a raven".*

Hint: In Welsh, "arth" means bear!

This painting was especially commissioned by the author to be painted by the British wildlife artist, Ben Waddams!

"The Crux of Arthurian Canon", by Ben Waddams

You can buy prints of this at www.habspruch.com

Chapter One

Introducing this Adventure!

The Secret Cypher of Edward the Confessor's Deathbed Dream

Edward the Confessor

Edward the Confessor was the King of England from the 8th of June, 1042, to when he died on the 5th of January, 1066.

Later, in the same year, William the Conqueror invaded Britain and took the Crown of England for himself—who defeated the English at the Battle of Hastings.

It is as though William the Conqueror had "cut down the **Great Old British Oak**".

This imagery is significant because, on Edward's deathbed, he had a prophetic dream about 'the restoration of a great tree that was cut down'.

Edward the Confessor's Deathbed Dream can be paraphrased as:

- In the dream, two Benedictine Monks whom Edward had previously known in Normandy came to him and pronounced that 'because of England's great sins, a great tree would be cut down, and at a distance of three furlongs, green branches would reattach themselves to the roots of the tree and flourish by their own accord'.

Significantly, Edward the Confessor is a saint in the Roman Catholic Church, as well as the Church of England; he is the only king of England to have ever been canonised by the Pope!

With such a saintly profile, Edward the Confessor's Deathbed Dream is considered to have been prophetic, and as you will discover, its interpretation is not only exciting, but it has a continuing bearing upon the age that we live in—and the age to come!

So, if William the Conqueror 'cut down the Great Old British Oak' in 1066, how long would it be before 'green branches would reattach themselves to the tree's roots and flourish by their own accord'?

It is quite clear that from 1066, the Great Old British Oak was felled and lay there in a forlorn barren state for quite a number of years—but for how many years?

The dream tells us that it was barren for 'three furlongs'—but that is how far an oxen would plough a field before turning around the other way—back in 1066, a 'furlong' was a long furrow!

As it turns out, the fulfilment of this prophecy would be scintillating!

The Bigger Picture

In this book, we treat Edward the Confessor's Deathbed Dream as a Secret Cypher that we will resolve to such a scintillating magnitude that many historians will be flabbergasted by its resounding truth!

In that context, you, as a Secret Cypher Super Sleuth, will also be opened up to opportunities to contribute to this topic's ongoing broader fulfilment. If you want 'leading-edge' capability, then 'be on the leading edge'—and here you are!

So, if you consider yourself to be a "Cypher"—that 'grey' name that we Secret Cypher Super Sleuths apply to ourselves in our merry ambition to 'play the grey man' whilst engaging with others in our grand adventures—then ask yourself this: "What epic might you be able to create upon this new knowledge of The Secret Cypher of Edward the Confessor's Deathbed Dream having been solved?"

This is not mere rhetoric designed to excite you as you continue to read about an exciting discovery. Instead, it is designed to make you conscious that opportunities will exist because of this discovery so that you can impact this new area of research as it unfolds towards its fulfilment—and this should enable you to acquire additional benefits in the process!

So, what doorway are you stepping through as you continue to read on?

Naturally, the opportunities available to any particular reader will depend not just on their circumstances but also on their capacity to exploit this new field—as such, I'll give you a generic pointer, which is the following.

As you read on, don't just get excited about how scintillating this new topic is—try your best to treat it more than just entertainment, more than just education—try and make it your best endeavour to do something about it, to take advantage of it.

At the very least, this might influence how some of our readers write their essays at school. As a community of Cyphers, our capability to impact those around us should naturally increase. Some of you will even form Secret Cypher Super Sleuth Clubs!

Astute readers will also realise that although this series of children's books is being written to teach children about our heritage, I've also used language suitable for adults to read. You can even encourage your parents to read these books!

At the start of each chapter, you'll notice a "Flesch" Reading Ease Score at the bottom of the page. I try to write at a level of about 65—this is about the same level as Readers Digest Magazine; the higher the number, the easier it is to read, and the lower the number, the harder it is to read. As it turned out, this book ended up being slightly more difficult at 50.

I use these numbers to try and balance my writings between "children who are aged 10 years plus and are enthusiastic advanced readers" and "adults who want the historical facts from a community leader but without the politics that deep-seated ethnic heritage often evokes".

Because of this, some of our readers will also be adults who will also be able to exploit these new discoveries to their advantage!

- This might be in the area of blogging or vlogging about a particular aspect of the newly emerging field of this discovery.

- It might be in writing books like I am, or even magazine articles.
- It might be as a community leader like me, raising the profile of the **marginalised**, the **suppressed**, and the **obfuscated** heritage of our indigenous Briton country folk.
- It might be as a teacher introducing this new knowledge to their students.
- Or it might be in how they are able to use this new knowledge to further those politics that help us, their fellow country folk.

So my generic "one size fits all" suggestion is that as you progress, that you keep in mind that some of these new ideas will lead you to new opportunities, which means that this book is more than just being about entertainment and education!

Perhaps the first common opportunity relates to everyone having plenty of people around them—so why not store up a series of "Do you know that ... ?" questions and see where they lead?

Write your own list of "Do you know?" questions and compose a three-minute speech on each topic! **I have!**

You can even practice these three-minute speeches in your Secret Cypher Super Sleuth Club and critically encourage each other to improve! **Play hard**, **learn hard!**

As time passes, your oral storage of these literary compositions will increase, and who knows, you may eventually have enough broad cross-sectional substance to write speeches, even your own book!

Becoming an expert is in your hands, no-one else's!

So, keep in mind the proverb, "As iron sharpens iron, so one man sharpens another!"—as such, you should value all of the responses to these questions and see how some of these engaging conversations increase your own substance, stature, and prevailing opportunities!

To enable you to take these matters further, I'll briefly talk about the Science of Secret Cyphers: this is the doorway that will open you to your own new personal adventures as we all walk down this same corridor of new emerging opportunities!

The premises are these:

1. Solving Secret Cyphers creates newly available information.
2. Newly available information opens doors to new topics of research.
3. New topics lead to new opportunities.
4. The exploiting of new opportunities brings additional benefits.
5. Additional benefits translate to your own increased prosperity.

To inspire you to move forward, I'd like to point out that in 2001, the Englishman of Trinidadian descent, *Sir Vidiadhar Surajprasad Naipaul,* won the **Nobel Prize in Literature** "for having united perceptive narrative and incorruptible scrutiny in works that compel us to see the presence of suppressed histories".

Although this is quite a complicated description, it really boils down to Sir Vidiadhar (pronounced 'Sir Vid-EE-ar Nye-Paul') having excelled in raising the ethnic identities of his own heritage, which had been suppressed by multiculturalism, into general public consciousness.

It suggests that Sir Vidiadhar skilfully combined a keen understanding of human experiences and events with a critical perspective, shedding light on aspects of history that have been deliberately ignored or marginalised.

His writing is praised for its ability

to captivate readers while also challenging them to confront uncomfortable truths and consider alternative perspectives on the past.

*What things have been **marginalised**, **suppressed**, or **obfuscated** in your ethnic background?*

In my own endeavours, I am focusing on raising the profile of the **marginalised**, the **suppressed**, and the **obfuscated** *heritage* of indigenous Britons and native Britain.

- Obviously, the revival of obfuscated heritage poses the challenge of "How can we shed light on the obscured—how do we restore 'the invisible' to once again being visible?"

Fortunately, I have identified an allegorical solution that might be compared to what some modern-day scientists might call "Discovering the Cosmic Microwave Background of the Universe".

Don't be put off by this term; it just means "discovering the cooled remnant of the first light that could ever travel freely throughout the Universe".

Let me explain this!

As it turned out, a special breed of scientists once discovered that no matter which direction they looked into the dark night sky, they could always see remnants of light that had travelled billions of years across space, which, being so old, could only have come from the early universe!

You can imagine this as if someone had lit a candle on the other side of the universe when the universe was just created, and you—on this other side of the universe, 13.5 billion years later, now looked out of your window and saw the light of that candle finally reaching earth!

What you would be seeing is real light that has crossed the universe to greet you—NOT something that is invisible!

So, what is the allegory here? Well, for a start, "we should look into the darkness of night for the most dim light that is, nevertheless, actual light that has travelled the ages to greet us"—what is this allegorical 'light'?

Because this 'light' is so old, we should also realise that, in literary terms, it is part of the "heritage" of the universe.

This is where we can pick up a little speed because—once again, in literary terms—"light" can be represented as "language that exposes truth".

We know this from cartoons, where a light bulb turns on in a thought bubble to tell us that the cartoon character has just realised something!

This is actually a visual, literary allegory that says that information can be regarded as light! It is as though 'information lights up the darkness of where information is absent'!

The parallel with the 'Cosmic Microwave Background' allegory is that in literary terms, *language* that has come down to us as part of our heritage is just like the light that comes to us from the early universe!

The big question is, "What does the **language of our early ancestors** tell us about that which has been obfuscated—'made invisible'?"

Although some of our heritage has been made invisible, the **language** that comes down to us—just like the light from the early universe—can still be seen!

So here's the News Flash!

The literary equivalent of astronomy's Cosmic Microwave Background are the Secret Cyphers broadcast to us by our ancestors from the ancient world—that's where 'our universe' first began!

- All we have to do is solve the Secret Cyphers of our ancestors, and what has been **suppressed**, **marginalised**, and **obfuscated** will not just be made visible again but will shine as brightly as they once did!

The exciting thing is that some of this heritage is not like a dim candle once lit on the other side of the universe, but is as bright as the shining sun in the clear blue sky!

To bring this to a crescendo, my open challenge to all of my readers is this:

- Who of you will grow up to be awarded a Nobel Prize in Literature that is based upon your capacity to both discover and resolve ancient Secret Cyphers that reintroduce **marginalised**, **suppressed**, and **obfuscated** heritage to the modern world—"**M-S-O**"?

Because it is so important to reintroduce heritage that has been **marginalised**, **suppressed**, and **obfuscated**—which I exemplify as being called "**M-S-O**"—I've created a few campaign quips to reinforce how important M-S-O is:

- "Unlock What We Know with M—S—O"
- "Let Heritage Grow with M—S—O"
- "Heritage on Show with M—S—O"
- "Let Voices Grow with M—S—O"
- "Revive the Flow with M—S—O"
- "Bring Back the Glow with M—S—O"
- "From Long Ago with M—S—O"
- "Sow seeds of revival with M—S—O"

We can also assert the relevance of these more boldly:

- "M—S—O *echoes* from long ago!"
- "M—S—O *revives* the glow!"
- "M—S—O *recovers* what we

know!"
- "M—S—O *makes* history grow!"

And finally, let's examine the obvious "hierarchy-of-trove" Call-To-Action:

1. "M—S—O: **discover** the trove!"
2. "M—S—O: **reveal** the trove!"
3. "M—S—O: **reclaim** the trove!"
4. "M—S—O: **explore** the trove!"
5. "M—S—O: **revive** the trove!"
6. "M—S—O: **cherish** the trove!"
7. "M—S—O: **treasure** the trove!"
8. "M—S—O: **celebrate** the trove!"

We are more than mere literary archaeologists—some of us are predestined to become the Indiana Joneses of our age!

And although I'm not campaigning to elevate myself into a distinguished position in the public eye, I do wonder about which of my readers will inevitably do so if they grasp the importance of M-S-O and promote it—as exemplified by Sir Vidiadhar

Naipaul winning the Nobel Prize in Literature in 2001 for doing just that!

So think about aiming well—and in doing so, aiming high!

I'll let you into a little secret: many British Prime Ministers made the decision that they would one day become Prime Minister when they were still children at Eton College.

1. Tomorrow's battleground is The Spoken Word, so today's decision should be to learn how to best wield 'the double-edged sword of truth'.
2. The Science of Secret Cyphers is your tool-kit.
3. How high you aim is up to you!
4. Your treasure-trove will be the hoard of M-S-O that you *rediscover*—Step 1 in that hierarchy!

So, I implore you to learn to become a master at solving Secret Cyphers!

Let me be your candle so that you can be the sun!

The Science of Secret Cyphers

I introduced the Science of Secret Cyphers in my previous book, "The Secret Cypher of Chalice Well", and although it would be helpful if you had read that book, I was mindful when writing this book that many readers will not have read the former book. Reading it is **not** a prerequisite!

For those who haven't read The Secret Cypher of Chalice Well but see themselves as part of a club whose members call themselves Cyphers, I recommend adding it to your reading list—it contains many sleuthing lessons about the Science of Secret Cyphers.

I will, for a moment, dwell on certain aspects of that book—not to promote the book, but instead to quote some useful examples from it!

Not only does The Secret Cypher of Chalice Well go into great depth about the Science of Secret Cyphers, but it resolves dozens of Secret Cyphers that are perhaps the closest ever to the British heart—and that is the exciting world of King Arthur!

What better introduction to Britain could there be but the capability to solve the Secret Cyphers of Arthurian Britain? I know of none better!

For example, you may have heard about The Lady of The Lake—which thus presents itself as "The Secret Cypher of the Lady of the Lake"— would you be surprised to learn that not only does this break down into two different Secret Cyphers, "The Secret Cypher of The Lady" and "The Secret Cypher of The Lake", these expose a third one, which appears as "The Secret Cypher **of the Relationship between** The Lady *and* The Lake"—which as it turns out, is The Secret Cypher of Evangelism?

As a mere illustration, this shows that one Secret Cypher can easily turn on a sixpence to actually be five Secret Cyphers juxtaposed in the same place!

The Science of Secret Cyphers involves many varied techniques and uses a language you might not be familiar with.

Because you might not have read The Secret Cypher of Chalice Well, I have added two special annexes at the end of this book:

- **"Annexe A: An Introduction to Cyphers"**. [Page 450] This annexe is actually Chapter One of that book in full (but with a few editing notes), which in that book is titled "An Introduction to Cyphers".
- **"Annexe B: An Introduction to Special Terminology"**. [Page 462] This annexe is a short but slightly edited excerpt from Chapter Eleven of that book, which introduced some

special terminology that I will continue to use in this book.

These annexes are merely a fast track into the science without having to read The Secret Cypher of Chalice Well!

Of course, you may not have to read those annexes, but you'll know that you especially need to dash across to Annexe B when you come across any of the following specialised words but don't know what they mean:

- Combobulate
- Decombobulate
- Combobulation
- Discombobulate
- Discombobulation
- and expressions such as "... and Bob's your uncle!", or words such as 'bob', and 'bobbin'.

Of course, those who have read The Secret Cypher of Chalice Well need not read those annexes, but as they are quite short, then reading them would be an excellent refresher for those who have already read them!

In fact, the only reason I have not included those annexes as chapters at the start of this book is that they would be repetitive for those who have already read Book #1 in this series.

Indeed, it is pretty likely that I will have to include those special annexes in every book that I write about Secret Cyphers—I have already planned Book #3 in this series, which is "The Secret Cypher of Why There Are Ravens in the Tower of London".

I do like a running start, but I don't want to compel you to need to read my other books to excel in each of these topics!

Inroad to Solving 'The Secret Cypher of Edward the Confessor'

One of the curious things about Edward the Confessor's Deathbed Dream of the year 1066 is that because it has a bearing upon our own modern age yet was written down almost a thousand years ago, we should first have suitable regard for the **prevailing context** of its imagery **at the time the dream occurred**.

Yet what is that prevailing context?

We get a glimpse of that from the following excerpt from my previous paraphrase of the dream:

- "… **a great tree** would be cut down, and at a distance of three furlongs, green branches would reattach themselves to the roots of the tree and flourish by their own accord'…"

Here, the prevailing context is the "Great Tree", whose roots dig down deeply into the annals of history before 1066, so profoundly that by this 'Age of Edward', the "Great Old British Oak" can be seen to be hundreds of years old.

Although I will expound on the whole dream later—that is, once we have all the nuts and bolts gathered around us 'as a series of bobbins that are ready to combobulate'—I'll first decypher the "Secret Cypher of the Great Old British Oak".

You'll quickly discover that this stage is a necessary precursor to interpreting the dream itself!

Then I'll get into the details of the actual dream, for example:

• How would "The Secret Cypher of Three Furlongs" decypher, which is evident in my paraphrase of the dream? And what about "The Secret Cypher of 'The Branches' of the Great Old British Oak"?

In decyphering the "Secret Cypher of the Great Old British Oak", I won't be as detailed in the depth of British history I explored in my book The Secret Cypher of Chalice Well.

However, I will still summarise around 12,500 years of British history in a single chapter—you'll find this in Chapter Three, which is then expounded further in future chapters—including investigating some additional nuances that weren't so relevant to the first book in this series.

With this as our merry backdrop, I'll then be able to press onwards toward my merry conclusion.

In pressing on, I'll not only get into the details of the original manuscript that recorded the dream but also how it affects King Charles III today!

Of course, if it affects King Charles, that begs the question, "How will it affect you and your descendants?"

If you have ever wanted a looking glass to the future, here it is!

"Mirror-mirror on the wall ..."...

Consider reading Annexes A and B from pages 450 and 462, NOW!

Chapter Two

The Secret Cypher of The Great Old British Oak

The First Secret Cypher of Many to Come!

It would seem that William the Conqueror cut down the "**Great Old British Oak**" in 1066. Yet, Edward the Confessor's preceding Deathbed Dream promised "... at a distance of three furlongs, green branches would reattach themselves to the roots of the tree and flourish by their own accord". The promise was that the tree would once again become itself!

Flesch—52; Reading time—7:45; Speaking time—14:54

- The dream was a prophecy about the future.
- As a promise, it was a message of hope. *But to whom?*

This promise supposed that the Great Old British Oak once took root, grew into a substantial tree, flourished for a time, was cut down, endured a period of 'interregnum' where no green branches sprouted from the stump, and finally, green branches were somehow 'reattached' to the tree—which then flourished by their own accord, so that in time the tree would become itself again!

Naturally, this Secret Cypher can be broken down into other Secret Cyphers. Because discoveries about each Secret Cypher will likely interleave with those of the others, a strict examination of each would be a good starting point.

On the subject of 'Secret Cyphers', we call them so because we wish to *rediscover* their lost meanings. There are, indeed, other terms that can also be applied to them—such as describing them as *kennings* or *circumlocutions*.

Both words, **kenning** and **circumlocution**, are effectively interchangeable, and that's because they represent the same literary phenomenon that existed in all three of Old Norse, Old English, and Old Welsh.

An example of an Old English kenning is *hronrad*, from "hron-rad" ('whale-road'), which means "sea". Somebody hearing *hronrad* would have understood that 'sea' was expressed despite *whale-road* being uttered.

I'll define both here:

- **Kenning:** a compound expression in Old English, Old Norse, and Old Welsh with metaphorical meaning, e.g. whale-road = sea.
- **Circumlocution:** a style of speak-

ing used to convey meaning indirectly so that *the listener* infers the meaning.

Naturally, these words have broader meanings when used in other contexts.

However, you should easily see how they converge on Welsh Expressions of Awen, such as "Great Arthurian Forrest", "Oaken Tree", "Great Old British Oak", and subsets of them—such as "The Roots" of The Great Old British Oak, "The Trunk",—etcetera.

Having given you the Old English example of *hronrad*—"whale-road" meaning 'sea'—, I should also give you an Old Norse and an Old Welsh example.

In Old Norse, the kenning *hrafnsauga* translates as "raven-eye" to mean the "sun".

And in Old Welsh, the kenning *Eryr*

y mynydd translates as "eagle of the mountain" to mean "powerful or majestic warrior".

The difference between a Secret Cypher and a kenning (or circumlocution) is that the meaning of the kenning is known, whereas despite that a Secret Cypher is also a kenning or circumlocution, it also conveys the additional context that its intended meaning has yet to be rediscovered.

For example, although the English word 'Merlin'—expressed in Old Welsh as 'Myrddin'—translates into the kennings (or circumlocutions) of 'sea-hawk' and 'sea-fortress,' as a Secret Cypher, we ponder why 'Myrddin', the title of a chief druid, would be metaphorically represented as a sea-hawk.

One can only suppose that this kenning related to a corresponding kenning—such as "Mor glas dyfn"—where despite this translating as 'deep blue

33

sea' would be a kenning that meant "the knowledge of all mankind": this does, of course, represent one of the roles of an arch druid—"to preserve in our peoples the knowledge of all mankind"—as such, the Chief Druid as a 'sea-hawk', a 'sea-fortress', would attract that title as a name when he is raised into that office.

Similarly, the name *Arthur* can be seen as a kenning, which, when treated as a Secret Cypher, can be seen to broadly mean "Bear-Warrior"—he would similarly attract that name as a title when raised into the lofty office of defending the heritage of Britain 'as a bear would', even to the death!

I even take this further in my book *The Secret Cypher of Chalice Well,* where I break down the broad kenning of Arthur, *bear-warrior*, into its probable origin of *bear-south* or *bear-right*, doing so based upon suitable Old Welsh etymologies where the direction of the south was where our ancient ancestors believed that *inspiration* (hence leadership) came from—and how the south relates to the right is because when one faces the east, the south is to one's right!

So, let's consider how the Secret Cypher of The Great Old British Oak can be broken down into multiple Secret Cyphers!

We can use these Cyphers as a guide to chart the next few chapters.

These Cyphers aren't just a simplistic breakdown of what a tree is composed of but are an array of interleaved complex ideas that can be easily grouped into various familiar contexts, viz-a-viz the following kennings:

1. The Secret Cypher of "**The Soil**" that The Great Old British Oak is Rooted In;
2. The Secret Cypher of "**The Roots**"

of The Great Old British Oak;

3. The Secret Cypher of "**The Trunk**" of The Great Old British Oak;

4. The Secret Cypher of "**The Branches**" of The Great Old British Oak; and,

5. The Secret Cypher of "**The Fruit**" of The Great Old British Oak - its crop of acorns.

As tokens of common symbols, these Secret Cyphers each have regard for the following:

1. The historical circumstances that The Great Old British Oak was rooted in, represented by "The Soil" having regard for 12,500 years of British history;

2. The historical circumstances that can be represented by "The Roots" of The Great Old British Oak, how they took root in "The Soil", and indeed, where those roots came from;

3. The 'divine right' of the tree to be a tree in the forest within which

it was rooted—represented by its trunk—alluding to the sovereign circumstances of the crown that prevails over the land which is beneath its canopy;

4. The historic and continuing reigns of consecutive kings over the land—represented by "The Branches" of The Great Old British Oak being personified as a collection of specific family tree 'branches' of each reigning king;

5. The prosperity of the land, represented by "The Fruit" of The Great Old British Oak—the acorns, which themselves fell and took root in the soil—which proffers an additional element that becomes a new Secret Cypher in itself:

6. The "Distribution and Destiny" of the land, as represented by those acorns taking root and flourishing, then seeding new trees from their own fruit taking root and flourishing.

Naturally, those who have read my

book, *The Secret Cypher of Chalice Well*, will have picked up on the phrase "Distribution and Destiny", and that's because of how a flourishing tree of The Great Arthurian Forrest can be seen as a product of that prosperity; I'll explain the unusual 'rr' spelling in the word 'forrest with a double-r', later—there are forests (with a single-r), and The Great Arthurian "Forrest" (with a double-r)—but just to whet your whistle, it has something to do with the word **druid** meaning 'oak-knower'!

Curiously, 'The Great Old British Oak' took root in 'The Great Arthurian Forrest'—it was just one of many 'oak trees'—so the retelling of its history has to account for what the symbolism of an oak tree meant **at the time** that 'The Great Old British Oak' laid down its 'roots' in 'the soil' that was common to all of these '*oaken trees*'.

Given that "... green branches would reattach themselves to the roots of

the tree and flourish by their own accord..." one can surmise that a pro-
spective 'return to Camelot' should
have something to do with not just
how the 'prosperity of the land' is
distributed, but also how the governance of such a 'Camelot' would affect our **destiny**.

In child-speak, this relates to how we
share things amongst ourselves and
how we organise ourselves.

Such a concept of '**Distribution and
Destiny**' needs to account for the
context of 'the tree' growing in an
environment that accommodates
"The Four Great Prophecies of Arthurian Britain"—so with the risk that interpreting the dream without these
might create an enigma, we would
also need to examine those!

Britain's history goes back to the melt
of the last ice age, around 12,500
years ago. In the next chapter, we
will look at "The Secret Cypher of The

Soil", in which 'The Great Old British Oak' is rooted.

This will give us a broad account of the last 12,500 years of British history—but not as a potted history in the sense of retelling a series of mere facts, but in the cherry-picking of those facts that collectively interleave to illustrate how The Great Old British Oak was once betrothed to be the bride of this land.

This 'Great Old British Oak' is, of course, "Britannia"—she is the national personification of Britain, who we know as a helmeted female warrior who holds a trident and shield!

Of course, I realise that this personification of Britannia has existed across many different ages—some of which included different levels of foreign occupation—and this image of Britannia goes back to *at least* The Romans!

In the 2nd century AD, Roman Britannia came to be personified as a goddess, armed with a spear and shield and wearing a Corinthian helmet.

However, as an indigenous Briton who is also a Christian who does not believe in such 'goddesses'—a trait that I share with the prominent 6th-century Celtic bard, Taliesin, who mentions Christ in his tome "The Battle of The Trees"—I have to contend that as the etymology of the word "Britannia" goes back to at least the 4th century BC, then the 'personification' of Britannia must go further back— and at least to our Celtic birth, at that!

This raises an interesting question— when was she born?

Because we can't prove that she was actually personified in the minds of our ancient ancestors way back then, and yet she can at the very least be personified in our own minds by us thinking of her as having been born back then—we must ask ourselves the following question:

- "What would be the earliest time we can identify such unity amongst our native ancestors of Britain that we can rightly personify that unity as being 'Britannia'?"

I would think that, at the very least, it must have been by the time that the leaders of this land started meeting centrally to make those oaths between each other that started characterising the existence of a common nature between us all—sometime in our pre-Roman very distant past.

At the least, our valiant warrior Britannia has weathered many ages over millenniums—if even just in our minds!

So, at the very worst, do we have the liberty to personify Britannia as having been born so far back, ourselves?

Of course, we do—we are the heirs of our ancient ancestors, and as heirs, we become them—so, when we speak with their authority, their authority has spoken!

Naturally, because the fulfilment of Edward the Confessor's Deathbed Dream relates to our own destiny, we can only wonder how prosperous we shall be in times to come!

The fulfilment of the dream does, at face value, promise newly founded prosperity in Britain!

So, how shall our dear Britannia be transformed from as if dressed in the linen of the modern age to being dressed in the finely woven golden fleece of her destiny?

She has, in a sense, been walking a fashion parade of the ages—what joy will she bring to us over the following few chapters as we walk down the corridors of time with her?

Read on, dear time traveller—doing so as if you were Lady Britannia herself peering into her golden looking glass with complete admiration:

"Mirror mirror on the wall,
Who's the fairest of them all?"

Chapter Three

The Secret Cypher of The Soil

12,500 Years of British History in a Single Chapter!

An explanation of the historical circumstances that 'The Great Old British Oak' was rooted in, represented by "The Soil" having regard for 12,500 years of British history.

Since the melt of the last ice age, Britain's **history** can be described as "The Soil" in which "The Great Arthurian Forrest" is rooted. The spelling with an 'rr' is intentional.

This is because "The Ascent of Arthurian Britain" can be traced as far back as 12,500 years, with various symbols compounding one upon the

Flesch—45; Reading time—1:04:00; Speaking time—2:04:00

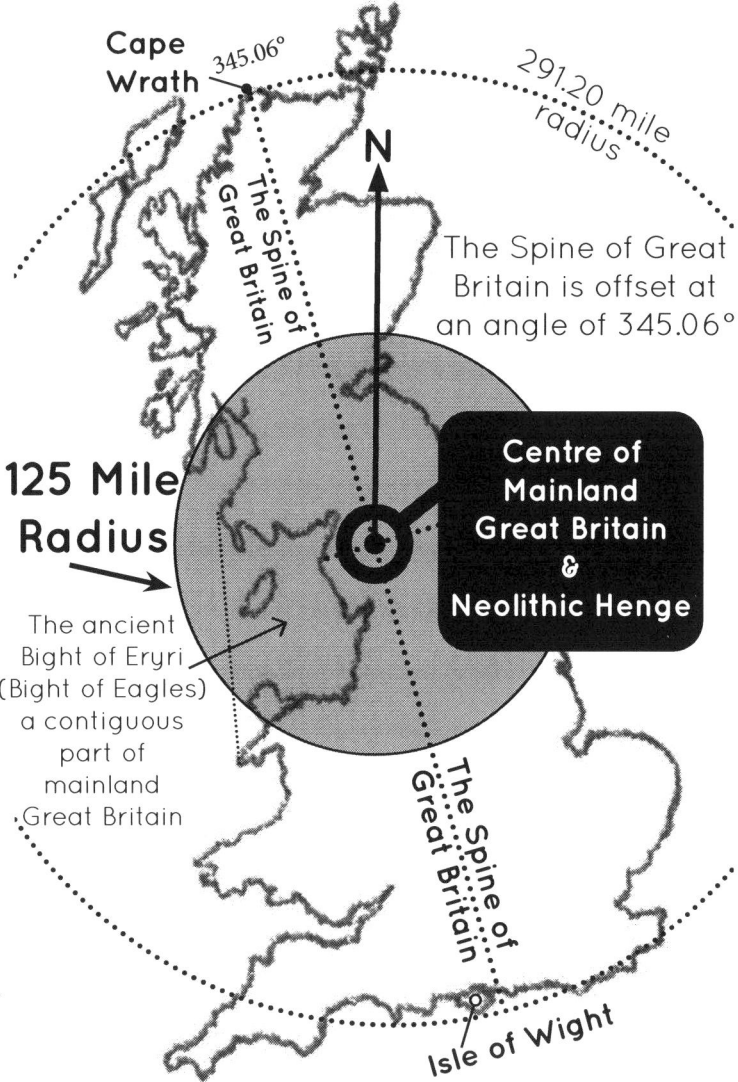

Cape Wrath

345.06°

291.20 mile radius

N

The Spine of Great Britain

The Spine of Great Britain is offset at an angle of 345.06°

125 Mile Radius

Centre of Mainland Great Britain & Neolithic Henge

The ancient Bight of Eryri (Bight of Eagles) a contiguous part of mainland Great Britain

The Spine of Great Britain

Isle of Wight

THE CENTRE OF MAINLAND GREAT BRITAIN

The mathematics of these calculations—including latitudes and longitudes—were published in my book "The Secret Cypher of Chalice Well".

46

other to become the 'Arthurian Britain' we know today.

The history I'll describe took place within a general 125-mile radius of a neolithic henge located 1.2 miles south of the centre of Penrith.

Although this neolithic henge did not exist 12,500 years ago, it boasts various characteristics that are significant to the story of any period.

Firstly, this neolithic henge is located at the exact centre of mainland Great Britain. As such, its **location** is a valuable central reference point when discussing anything about the history of mainland Great Britain.

History related to the centre of Great Britain is generally relevant to all parts of Great Britain—what generally happened in the centre most likely happened elsewhere—or at least had a similar bearing as many other places in Britain.

The Near Past—Around 2,000 BC to the Present Day

The henge was created around 4,000 years ago, and its purpose was to be the Chief Meeting Place of the Leaders of Britain.

Even the Kingdom of England was created at this henge in 926 AD, when various kings of Britain met to declare their oaths to the King of Wessex in a triumphant act that formally created England.

Going back to "The Age of Arthur"—which is generally accepted to have been between 350 and 650 AD—this neolithic henge was at the exact centre of that broad radius of 125 miles from it, which is now remembered in Welsh as Yr Hen Ogledd: "The Old North".

The 'Age of Arthur' embraces the decline of the Roman Empire to when the Romans left Britain in 410 AD.

It includes the re-formation of native kingdoms within that broad radius of 125 miles under Coel Hen, who was the last *Dux Britanniarum*—Duke of Britain—which gives rise to the notional name of the region being the "Duchy of Britain".

It includes the rise of the Anglo-Saxons around 449 AD, which led to 'King Arthur' opposing them, who is thought to have died at the Battle of Camlann in 537 AD.

It then includes the "Age of Heroism", which started around 530 AD when Urien, King of Rheged, The Old North's most famous king, came of age—his court included the famous bards Taliesin and Aneirin. This heroic age came to a swift end in the year 638 AD when Urien's great-granddaughter, Princess Rhiainfellt, the heiress Queen of Rheged, married the Anglo-Saxon prince Oswiu of Bernicia.

The marriage of Rhiainfellt, Queen of

THE AGE OF ARTHUR 350 - 650 AD

Including its
Pre-Arthur ascent,
Post-Arthur "Age of
Heroism", then decline!

Nicene Christianity declared
State Religion of Roman Empire

43AD to 410AD

Romans

Magnus Maximus

350

378+

380

388   ? died

Sarmatians
at Ribchester
with Dragon
pennants for
10+ generations,
Best
Horsemen
of Their Age

transition of power

**Appointed by
Magnus Maximus
(Duke of Britain)**

**Coel Hen
Dux Britanniarum
(Duke of Britain)**

410   died

Romans left Britain

449   ?

?

White Dragon

**Anglo-
Saxon
buildup**

Why?

Arthur

Fighting
for the Red
Dragon

510   c.530

Best Horsemen
of This Age   ?

Men of The North

Ceneu
Ledlum
Meirchion
Cynfarch

**Urien
of Rheged**

Senior Kingdom
In Yr Hen Ogledd

537?

585   Y Gododdin

600

**THE AGE OF HEROISM
c. 530 - 638 AD**

Urien's Coming of Age
until the marriage of his
great granddaughter.
Includes bards such as
Taliesin and Aneirin!

Rhun
Rhoeth   Owain
Kentigern

Rheged

Carvetii tribe

from time
immemorial

638 ... 650

Anglo

**Rhiainfellt
of Rheged
married
Oswiu
of Bernicia**

Decline with reali-
sation that Rheged
served Angles

Hope!

to Celtic
present

duel

2022
...

50

©

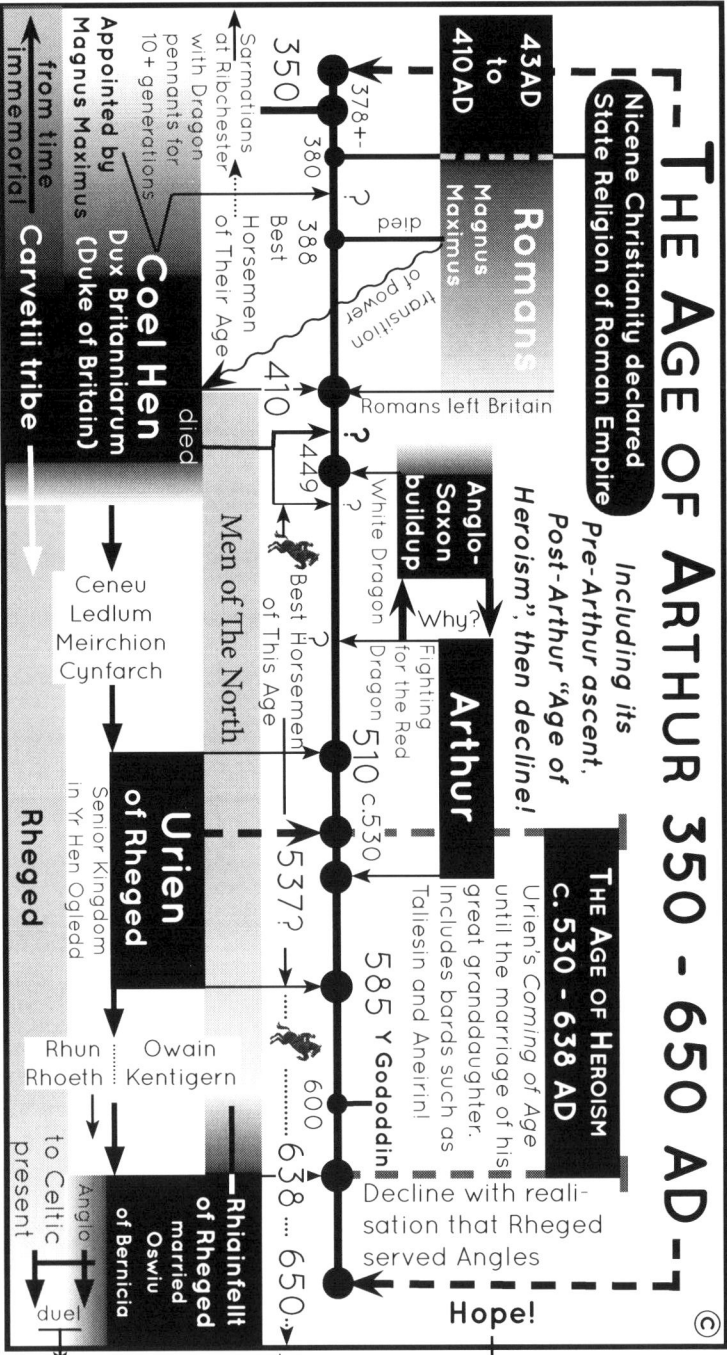

Rheged, to Oswiu, a prince of Bernicia and brother of the 6th Anglo-Saxon High King, led to the decline of the Age of Arthur by the year 650.

That Coel Hen was the last Dux Britanniarum effectively continued the Roman practice of administering Britain from the centre of mainland Great Britain, which is marked by that ancient henge at its very centre.

Although the Romans' administration of Britain from mainland Great Britain's *centre* would have come down from the Romans' appreciation of the strategic benefits of doing so, the matter that they did so was in continuance of the more ancient Briton practice of doing the same thing before the Romans arrived.

The indigenous Briton characteristic of Britain being governed from the centre of mainland Great Britain is exemplified by the henge's strategic location at the centre of mainland

THE DESCENT OF THE MEN OF THE NORTH

Bonedd Gwyr y Gogledd

Magnus Maximus `From Page 1`

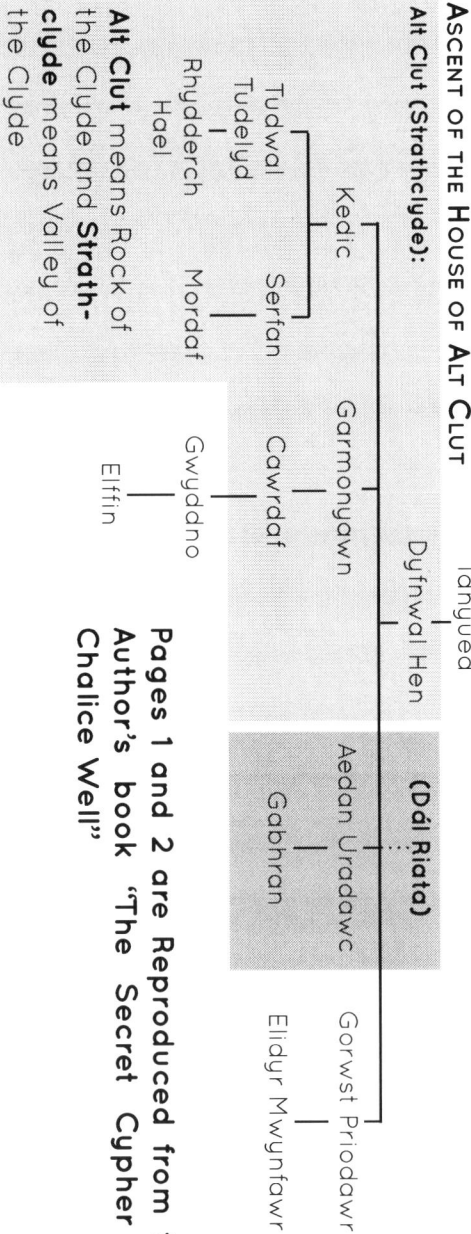

ASCENT OF THE HOUSE OF ALT CLUT

Idn:gued
Dyfnwal Hen
(Dál Riata)

ASCENT OF THE HOUSE OF ALT CLUT
Alt Clut (Strathclyde):

Kedic
Tudwal Tudclyd
Serfan
Rhydderch Hael
Mordaf

Garmonyawn
Cawrdaf
Gwyddno
Elffin

Aedan Uradawc
Gabhran
Gorwst Priodawr
Elidyr Mwynfawr

Alt Clut means Rock of the Clyde and **Strathclyde** means Valley of the Clyde

Pages 1 and 2 are Reproduced from the Author's book "The Secret Cypher of Chalice Well"

THE DESCENT OF THE MEN OF THE NORTH

ASCENT OF THE HOUSE OF RHEGED

Bonedd Gwyr y Gogledd

- The senior kingdom, both geographically and by inheritance.
- Kingdoms were often split between sons.

Rheged:
Gorwst
Letlwm
Meirchiawn
Cynfarch — Eidyr Lydanwyn
Urien — Llywarch Hen

Rheged means gift, or gifted prosperity

Coel ◄········· **Magnus Maximus**

Appointed Coel the last Dux Britanniarum

See Page 2

Roman Emporer, his death in 388AD marked the end of direct imperial presence in Britain

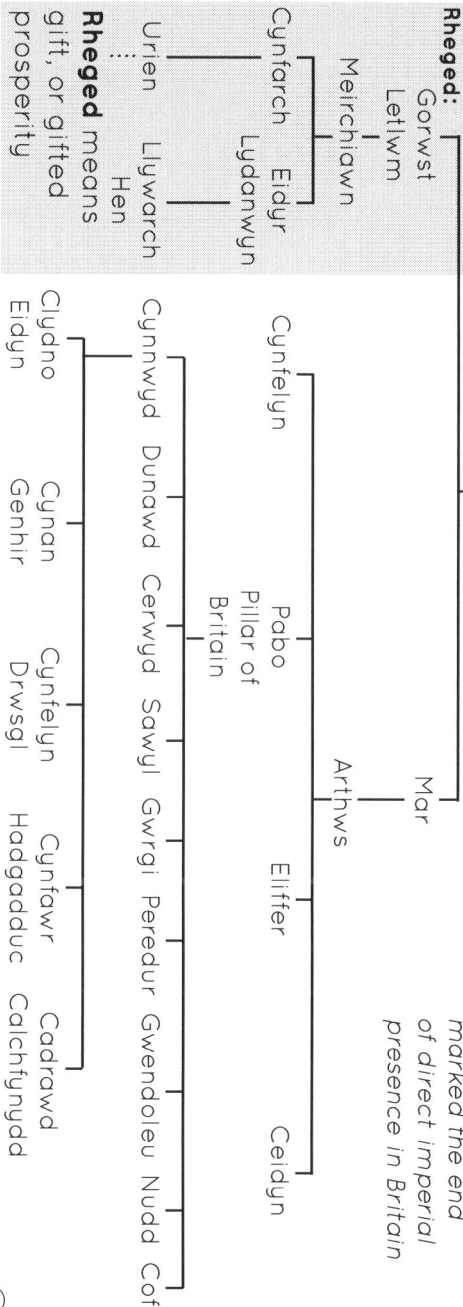

Ceneu

Mar — Arthws

Pabo Pillar of Britain — Eliffer

Cynfelyn

Cynnwyd — Dunawd — Cerwyd — Sawyl — Gwrgi — Peredur — Gwendoleu — Nudd — Cof

Ceidyn

Clydno Eidyn — Cynan Genhir — Cynfelyn Drwsgl — Cynfawr Hadgadduc — Cadrawd Calchfynydd

©

53

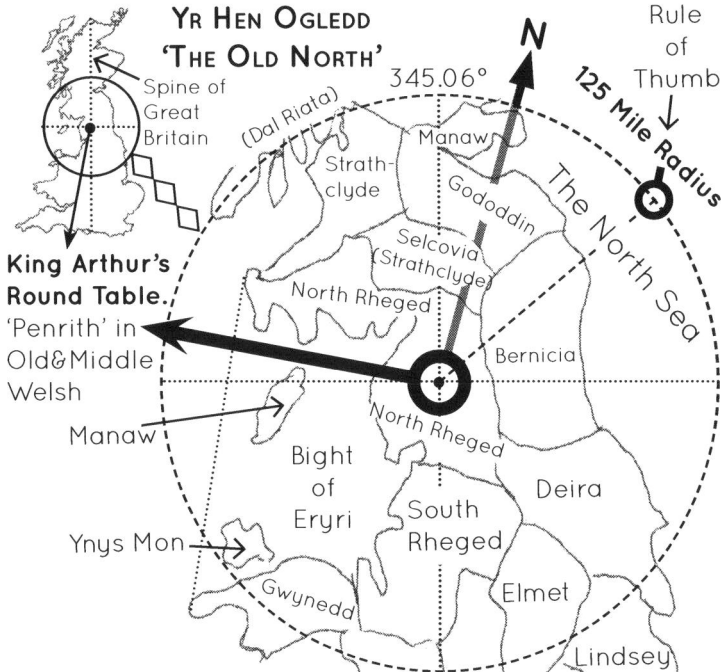

YR HEN OGLEDD
'THE OLD NORTH'

Spine of Great Britain

(Dal Riata)

345.06°

N

Rule of Thumb

125 Mile Radius

The North Sea

Manaw

Strath-clyde

Gododdin

Selcovia (Strathclyde)

North Rheged

King Arthur's Round Table..
'Penrith' in Old&Middle Welsh

Bernicia

Manaw

North Rheged

Bight of Eryri

South Rheged

Deira

Ynys Mon

Gwynedd

Elmet

Lindsey

Post 410 AD but illustrating Anglo-Saxon king-doms that later took hold in Yr Hen Ogledd
Borders and radii are stylistic approximations,
e.g. Gwynedd is entirely inside Yr Hen Ogledd

History of 'The Old North'

This region was largely born out of ancient Briton regions regaining control of the former region of the Roman Empire that was under the command of the Dux Britanniarum. the Duke of Britain. The kingdoms trace their roots back to Coel Hen, the Old King Cole of our nursery rhymes!

54

Great Britain, but doing so under notions of its central location conflating with the henge having the purpose of being the **Chief Meeting Place of the Leaders of Britain** "where they would make **oaths** between one and another".

Here, the practice of the Leaders of Britain collectively making oaths between one and another at this central henge effectively "laid down a 'distributed constitution'" that prevailed over how Britain was regionally governed.

As such, Britain was effectively demonstrated as "subject to the sum of those oaths" that all of the distributed leaders had collectively made in this central location.

Mainland Great Britain is actually quite a small isle—it has a radius of only 291.20 miles from its geographic centre at the henge. It was the collection of oaths that all of the regional Leaders of Britain undertook at that central henge that formalised the sense of what it was to be a Briton—which itself had been formulated by the collective history of this isle.

The essence of this is that those who made those oaths at the henge had inherited a legacy from as far back as the melt of the previous ice age, and this guided the 'prevailing **hand**' of their decision-making when undertaking those oaths at the henge!

But what does this mean?

Curiously, this region is now remembered in the native language of this land as Yr Hen Ogledd—which the English typically translate as "The Old North"—yet the inherent paradox of how "The Old Centre" became notionally translated as "The Old North" is revealed in the history of the evolution of the etymology of the unmutated form of this word, Gogledd.

Although Gogledd is typically translated as "left, north", its etymology was first attested in the 12th Century as the following:

- **Gogledd**: formed as go- ("**under**") + cledd ("**left hand**", "left side"), the north being on the left-hand side when facing east (similarly, compare de ("right", "south")).

In this sense, Yr Hen Ogledd better translates as "being under the (left) hand of **the law**"—under the 'prevailing **hand**'—and here, the historical context of "the left" being an allegory for 'the law' is probably best expressed by the Christian notion where Christ said, "Do not think that I have come to abolish the Law or the Prophets; I have not come to abolish them but to fulfil them." (NIV)

Although this is easily illustrated by Christ "sitting at the right hand of the Father"—hence God sitting on Christ's **left** represents **The Laws** of God—these notions are also reflected in expressions of modern-day politics where "The **legislative** canvas of 'The Left' contrasts with the action-driven palette of 'The Right'".

By the time of the decline of the Roman empire, these legacies were firmly placed in the hands of Coel Hen—the "Old King Cole" of our nursery rhymes—who is thought to have been appointed by Magnus Maximus, the last Roman Emperor to exercise any direct imperial control over Britain and who died in 388 AD.

The Romans didn't call their prevailing leader the Duke of *Central* Britain; they called him The Duke of Britain—to control the centre of Britain was to control Britain itself!

Indeed, as the history of this period shows, to control the Kingdom of Rheged—which contains the henge—was to control Yr Hen Ogledd, and to control Yr Hen Ogledd was to control Britain!

During the Roman administration of Britain, that part of the broader "Duchy of Britain" that contained this henge and later became Rheged was occupied by the Romans under a treaty with the local Carvetii tribe—whose deep roots go back to at least 9,000 BC, and this takes us back to a thousand years after the melt of the last ice age.

To put this in context, the modern-day County of Cumberland dates back to the kingdom of Rheged—whose kings were the senior line of Coel Hen—and Rheged itself dates back to the Carvetii, which effectively dates back to the melt of the last ice age!

With all this significance exuding from the centre of Britain out to all of its farthest reaches, what is this henge's name?

This henge's name is "**King Arthur's Round Table**".

In my book "The Secret Cypher of Chalice Well", I explained the mathematics behind this henge's location—including latitudes and longitudes—proving that this henge is at the exact centre of mainland Great Britain, with an accuracy that is under a quarter of a mile.

Indeed, to account for the erosion of the coastlines since the henge was created 4,000 years ago, I determined that The Spine of Great Britain must have protruded 2.69 miles past Cape Wrath's modern-day coastline in the north, yet just 2.43 miles south of the Isle of Wight at its southern end—and this compares very well with erosion rates over the last Century, which extrapolated backwards over 4,000 years, demonstrated a mean of 2.5 miles, verses my northern 2.69 and southern 2.43.

King Arthur's Round Table is indeed the centre of mainland Great Britain and can be demonstrated so to a very high level of accuracy!

I also went into great detail about how it was named in both Old Welsh and English and how significant it is to Britain's history.

If you are interested in the significance of this henge—or the whole Arthurian cycle—you should add that book to your reading list!

Just 1.2 miles north of King Arthur's Round Table is the centre of the market town of Penrith, whose name was first recorded in the 12th Century.

Although Middle Welsh is from the 12th to the 15th centuries, its predecessor, Old Welsh, was from around 800 AD until the 12th Century.

In Old Welsh, the idiom "Chief Meeting Place of the Leaders of Britain" translates into the word "Penrith", using the construct Pen + Rhith = Penrith.

Here, *Pen* means 'chief, head', and *rhith* means 'appearance', with *rith* being its soft mutation.

As a matter of Welsh *Awen*—'muse'— the expression "The Chief Appearing Place" transposes into the "Chief Meeting Place" of those who met there—who else would have taken oaths there but "Leaders of Britain"?

Although this substantially illustrates that the Old Welsh name for the henge was Penrith—having its linguistic roots somewhere between 800 AD and the 12th Century—one must realise that the henge was built long before the town of Penrith!

One can only suppose that over centuries—even millennia—the practice of the leaders of Britain meeting at the henge, having initially encamped northwards of the henge on that fell that is now known as Penrith Fell, led to how the fell got its name.

Then, over time, when various buildings were erected at the foot of that fell, the market town that we now know as Penrith rose to become the Penrith that we are so proud of today.

This strongly implies that the spelling of the name Penrith originated sometime between 800 AD and the 12th Century, having evolved from its previous Archaic Welsh between 550 AD and 800 AD, which itself evolved from Common Brittonic from the 6th Century, which in turn had evolved from Proto-Celtic from sometime in the middle of the first millennium BC.

This also means that the henge "King Arthur's Round Table" was likely known as "Penrith"—in some form of this word's development—during the Age of Arthur.

This also makes the Old Welsh name of the henge the primary candidate for the origin of the name of the market town of Penrith!

It is also a curious supposition that Arthur actually met with other leaders at the henge, and of the many reasons for supposing this, two stand out:

1. As exemplified by various kings having met at the henge in the year 926 to swear oaths of allegiance to the King of Wessex—upon which the creation of the Kingdom of England was formalised—the henge was known to already have pre-eminence as The Chief Meeting Place of the Leaders of Britain. Instead of those kings swearing allegiance at Winchester, the capital of the Kingdom of Wessex, they chose to do it at King Arthur's Round Table, which would have been known as Penrith during the Age of Arthur.

2. The henge is located on a geographic thoroughfare connecting mainland Great Britain's north

with the south. Most of the leaders of the Age of Arthur who travelled between the north and the south would have passed through Penrith: to any leader whose scope included the north and the south, *the henge*, known as a chief meeting place, would have been a regular part of their vernacular.

First of all, this shows how significant the English name of this henge is— King Arthur's Round Table. This name actually represents the truth of both the historical purpose of the henge and the likelihood that Arthur actually met with other Leaders of Britain at that henge!

As a historical monument, the henge "King Arthur's Round Table" effectively has pre-eminence over every other archaeological site in Britain!

This can be further characterised that by the time the name Penrith was recorded as a written word in the 12th

Century, the henge had seen many ages since the time it was built—in this sense, the henge is a strategic 'time-funnel' that collects all of the regional legacies of Britain into a single point, representing them all!

At the time of its construction, it had inherited the legacies of the preceding period, from the melt of the last ice age around 10,000 BC down to around 2,000 BC.

These legacies had matured by around 2,000 BC to the extent that the leaders of mainland Great Britain needed somewhere central to meet, where its leaders could make oaths between each other.

Having a formal "Chief Meeting Place of the Leaders of Britain" made oath-taking between leaders a formal matter of due course!

Of course, the creation of "Formality" among leaders was one of the most significant epochs of human history: civilisation without formality doesn't exist!

The henge itself was in good hands, as by the time the Romans came, the people of the region who were the guardians of the henge, the Carvetii, had become known as The Stag People, from the Brittonic word "carv", which means stag or deer.

The fact that these people were known as The Stag People is significant in itself—as we shall later discover, the Carvetii were the heirs of The Stag People of Star Carr, who, already by 9,000 BC, had adopted the stag symbol to represent the social clan-like structures that we are familiar with today.

The henge has since seen the rise and fall of the Roman Empire in Britain and the rise and decline of the Age of Arthur, including visits by many characters such as Arthur himself, as well as Urien, King of Rheged—who was also known as Urien, King of the Ravens—and his great-granddaughter, Princess Rhiainfellt, the last native Queen of Rheged.

From Rhiainfellt's dynastic marriage in 638 to Oswiu—who became the 7th Anglo-Saxon High King and who convened the Synod of Whitby, thereby creating the foundation of The Church of England in the process—the henge had seen the Kingdom of Rheged continuing as a native kingdom but articulated to the office of the Anglo-Saxon High King.

Here, we should pause to understand what it means for a state to be 'articulated' to another state!

Broadly, the word **articulated** means to connect one thing to another 'as if by a joint'. Take the concept of an *articulated lorry* as an example!

On the one hand, there is a lorry; on

the other hand, there is its trailer, and both are connected 'as if by a joint'.

In this description, the trailer is no less a trailer than as it was before it was connected to the lorry.

As such, the trailer has not blended to become part of the lorry—the *articulation* is the hinge that connects them! They both retain their separate identities!

That same trailer can be disconnected from the lorry and hooked to another lorry. Or it can be disconnected from the lorry and have its own power train built into it so that it can conduct its affairs without needing another lorry!

So, given that I have alluded to the Kingdom of Rheged being articulated to the Kingdom of England, one has to wonder what the form of the articulation is that does so!

The articulation that connects the Kingdom of Rheged to the Kingdom of England was the dynastic marriage between Rhiainfellt, Queen of Rheged, and Oswiu, of Bernicia, who was the brother of the 6th Anglo-Saxon High King.

That articulation—but subject to ethnic terms and conditions that made the Ravens of Rheged allegorical 'ravens'—put the Ravens of Rheged in allegiance with the Office of the Anglo-Saxon High King.

The Anglo-Saxons knew that to control Rheged was to control Yr Hen Ogledd, and to control Yr Hen Ogledd was to control Britain, so they held Rheged tightly to that office.

As we will discuss later, the people of Rheged were famed for being the "Ravens of Rheged" under Urien, who was known as King of the Ravens—and everyone knew that "ravens always get from one side of adversity to the other"!

This characteristic is exemplified by the matter that in the centuries before Christ, Celts were known to go to war under the sign of the raven. And we know what the symbol of the raven meant to the people of the Old World—just a token examination of the raven's role in the story of the Great Flood demonstrates this:

1. The raven's role is to get from one side of adversity to the other.
2. It is "the beating of the raven's wings that dries the flood waters from all the earth".
3. Once the raven has done its job, there can be new growth towards the forthcoming peace, over which the dove of peace prevails.

Points 1 and 2 are exemplified in Chapter 8 Verse 7 of the Book of Genesis, and Point 3 is exemplified by verses 8 to 11. I deep-dive into this in my book *The Secret Cypher of Chalice Well.*

71

So, no wonder Celts used to go to war under the sign of the raven—it was considered to be part of the holy order of things in the general perception of The Old World!

That is—" When encountering adversity":

- First, the Raven does its job.
- Then, the Dove of Peace is released.

So, given that the people of Rheged saw themselves as Ravens of Rheged, they believed they were predestined to get from one side of adversity to the other—the only question was, "When?"

The sum of this is that Rheged would never stop being itself—as an *articulated* state, it was nevertheless a state in its own right, but in this case, defined by the ethnicity of its people in that 'ravens' always get from 'one side of adversity to the other'.

Anything that was not represented as being equal on the 'other' side of the adversity as it was 'before the start' of the adversity would merely signify that Rheged was still under the duress of continuing to being in the central period of the adversity—but which adversity was predestined to eventually come to an end!

It was because Rheged had been articulated to the Office of the Anglo-Saxon High King that when the King of Wessex became the King of England—upon the oaths that were taken at the henge in the year 926—Rheged became articulated to the English crown down through the ages.

Indeed, the King of England marched into Rheged in 945 AD and claimed it by right!

By what right?

By the right of the dynastic marriage

between Rhiainfellt and Oswiu in 638 AD—which in that day was 'not long ago', only 307 years!

It should also be realised that to the Anglo-Saxon High Kings, the Kingdom of Rheged was not just one of the many states under his administration as High King: all of the prophecies related to both Rheged and its 'ravens' conflated to mean that the biggest risk to the Anglo-Saxon Heptarchy ever being defeated, broken up, and then expelled from Britain would be the poor administration of Rheged.

The danger was this:

1. If the 'ravens' of Rheged were ever released from the obligation of their loyalty to the Anglo-Saxon High King that they had acquired under the dynastic marriage of Rhiainfellt, Queen of Rheged, to Prince Oswiu of Bernicia—whose brother was the 6th Anglo-Saxon

High King—they would be able to revert to their prerogative of 'doing what ravens do' - and that would be to expel the Anglo-Saxons from Britain!

2. As such, the responsibility of the faithful administration of Rheged was elevated to the Office of the Anglo-Saxon High King: it was **he** who had the prevailing responsibility of defending the *whole* Anglo-Saxon Heptarchy!

Between Oswiu having been the 7th Anglo-Saxon High King and that fortuitous oath-taking ceremony at the henge in 926 AD, the kings of Wessex had come to dominate all of the Anglo-Saxon kingdoms that made up the Anglo-Saxon Heptarchy.

From that time, none of these kingdoms ever again broke away from the line of the High King—England's crown of today goes all of the way back to the kings of Wessex when Wessex was restored for the second time in 1042, under Edward the Confessor—and then, via the same line of the office of the Anglo-Saxon High King, the line of England's crown goes all of the way back to that dynastic marriage between the 'Ravens of Rheged' and the Anglo-Saxons, when Oswiu and Rhiainfellt wed.

At that time, Oswiu's brother, Oswald, was the 6th Anglo-Saxon High King— we will recount this lineage in Chapter 6.

So, in this 21st Century, King Charles had inherited not just the Kingdom of Rheged—but articulated to him under the name of the County of Cumberland—King Charles had also inherited the prevailing responsibility of defending the whole Anglo-Saxon realm from the possibility of 'The Ravens of Rheged' from being released from having the responsibility of serving the Anglo-Saxon crown.

Indeed, every king and queen before

Charles—all of the way back to both Oswald and Oswiu as the 6th and 7th Anglo-Saxon High Kings—has had the same responsibility!

The curious thing about Oswiu's lifetime is that all of the Anglo-Saxon High Kings, apart from the 1st and 2nd, were directly in his orbit, either by his own family having held the crown or he being connected by someone in relationship to a previous Anglo-Saxon High King.

In that sense, Oswiu was heavily endeared to what the Office of the Anglo-Saxon High King entailed and the implications of so being entailed!

Indeed, Oswiu's heritage is pivotal to so many things across Britain even today—to exemplify this, these even include every single Easter Church Service in the country, and that is because in 664, Oswiu ruled that Easter was to be conducted according to the Roman church's calendar, not the

Celtic church's calendar!

Not too many years after England was formed at the henge in 926 AD, the Kingdom of Rheged—but then known in Old English as Cumberland—was given to the King of Scots, but with the King of England remaining Cumberland's High King. This happened in 945 AD.

Although later kings of England ultimately regretted having given Cumberland to the King of Scots—which resulted in a quarrel between the English and Scottish kings that was really nothing more than a quarrel between the two kings that can be exemplified by the term "Cumberland Tennis".

This term illustrates *a chain of volleys between just the two players where both made their claims yet everyone else were merely innocent onlookers who were nevertheless obligated to respect the score*—Rheged was finally returned to England under the Treaty of York in 1237 AD.

This put the henge back under direct English control, which has continued to descend through the ages down to today—known by we natives as *Rheged* in Welsh, but by the English as the County of *Cumberland.*

The significance of this is that since the dynastic marriage of Rhiainfellt to Oswiu in 638 AD, the Anglo-Saxon and Rheged crowns have been as if 'two stars in a binary system' that would rotate around each other until one of these stars consumed the other.

According to The Four Great Prophecies of Arthurian Britain—which we will discuss after the next section—the Crown of Rheged would consume the English Crown, not the other way around! You'll be able to read about this scintillating topic in my next book in this series, *The Secret Cypher of Why There Are Ravens in the Tower of London.*

In light of this indigenous tenacity, the fascinating question is, "When the henge was first built, what did the people of this region inherit from the previous age before the henge was built—and what contribution did it make to the period of the whole life of the henge that we have just discussed?"

The Far Past—The Melt of the last Ice Age until around 2,000 BC

Creswell Crags is 114 miles from the henge—which being under 125 miles, means it is still within the region of Central Britain—and deep in a cave is an etching of "The Leftwards Facing Stag". It is dated to 10,500 BC.

The cave art at Creswell Crags depicts many animals, possibly including birds. Although most of these etchings have faded beyond any sense of comprehension, we do know from the diet of the people of Star Carr in later centuries that animals present in this broad region included Auroch (wild cow), Badger, Bear, Beaver, Birds, Elk, Hare, Hedgehog, Pine Marten, Red Deer, Roe Deer, and Wild Boar.

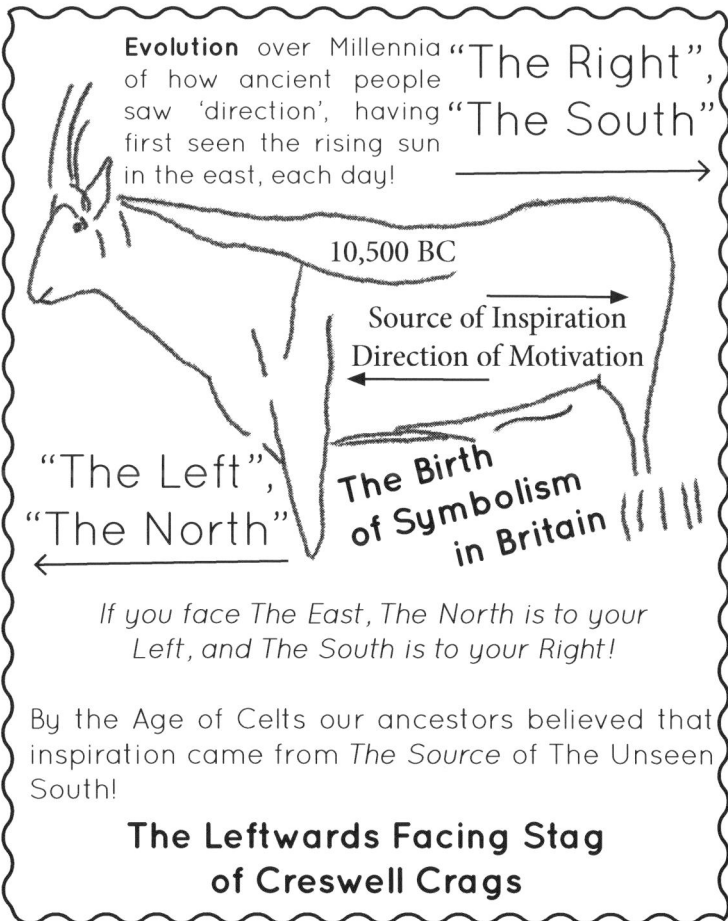

Evolution over Millennia of how ancient people saw 'direction', having first seen the rising sun in the east, each day!

"The Right", "The South"

→

10,500 BC

Source of Inspiration
Direction of Motivation

←

"The Left", "The North"

The Birth of Symbolism in Britain

←

If you face The East, The North is to your Left, and The South is to your Right!

By the Age of Celts our ancestors believed that inspiration came from *The Source* of The Unseen South!

The Leftwards Facing Stag of Creswell Crags

Curiously, out of all of the animals that were depicted in these cave etchings at Creswell Crags around 10,500 BC, it was reverence for the stag that had consolidated by around 9,000 BC to represent the social clan-like structures that we are familiar with today.

That would lead to the henge being built so that the leaders of Britain could gather to meet and make oaths between each other.

On the one hand, single clan-like social structures were represented by the symbol of the stag, yet cooperation between clans was undertaken by their "chief stags" making oaths to one another.

The curious question—and which has a scintillating answer—is this:

- How was the symbol of the stag transmitted down from the melt of the last ice age, and in particular, through the people of the

The Ancient Midlands of Britain

* Using naming conventions where 'Carria' derives from the Celtic 'Carv' for Stag, reminiscent of 'The Stag People' of Star Carr, and the later Carvetii Tribe who became Rheged

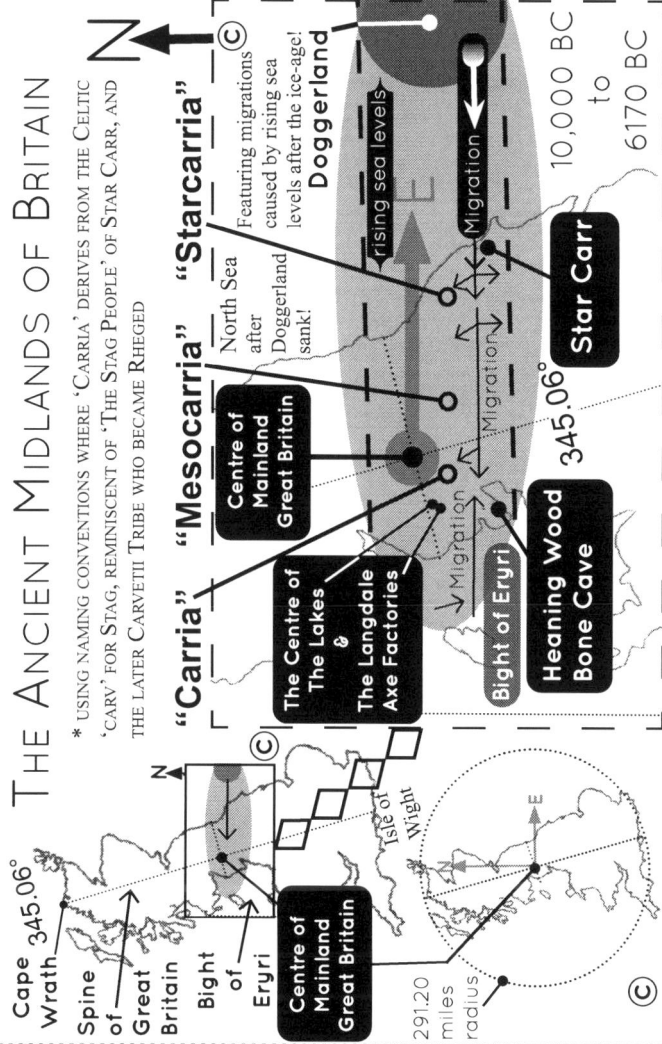

N

"Starcarria"

Featuring migrations caused by rising sea levels after the ice-age!

Doggerland

rising sea levels

Migration

Star Carr

10,000 BC to 6170 BC

"Mesocarria"

North Sea after Doggerland sank!

Centre of Mainland Great Britain

Migration

345.06°

"Carria"

The Centre of The Lakes & The Langdale Axe Factories

Bight of Eryri

Heaning Wood Bone Cave

Migration

At 9,000 BC, coastlines were perhaps a hundred miles further out to sea before the ice melted so far as to raise the sea levels towards their current state!

Present day coastlines!

Reproduced from the Author's book "The Secret Cypher of Chalice Well"

N

C

Cape 345.06° Wrath

Spine of Great Britain

Bight of Eryri

Centre of Mainland Great Britain

Isle of Wight

291.20 miles radius

E

C

The **"Stag People of Star Carr"** were the first known socially organised people in Britain, and their descendants were among those who built the henge called King Arthur's Round Table over 4000 years ago.

The 21 Stag Headresses discovered at Star Carr, which are 11,000 years old, show the beginning of clan-like social structures that had matured by the time King Arthur's Round Table was built so that leaders from all over Britain could meet!

Carvetii tribe who administered the henge—'The Stag People'— who later became the people of the Kingdom of Rheged, and then the people of the County of Cumberland?

Three major discoveries are relevant to answering this question:

1. **c. 9,000 BC.** Martin Stables recently discovered human remains in Heaning Wood Bone Cave, located just south of the lake, Windermere, in The Lake District, at Heaning Wood near Ulverston. Thousands of years later, the people in this region would become known as the Carvetii—The Stag People.
2. **c. 9,000 BC.** The discovery of 21 Stag Headdresses at Star Carr, located just over a hundred miles east of Heaning Wood and which settlement is known to have been occupied for at least 800 years.
3. **c. 10,000 - c. 6,170 BC.** The sinking of 'Doggerland' to the east of

Star Carr caused the mass migration of the peoples of Doggerland into "Starcarria", leading to some of "The Stag People of Star Carr" migrating westwards to the high ground of the Lake District, then being transmitted down through the ages, whose descendants became known as the Carvetii—The Stag People.

Star Carr is Britain's most important Mesolithic site, boasting the earliest known carpentry in Europe!

Significantly—and despite the distance of around a hundred miles between them—the peoples around both Heaning Wood and Star Carr came to share a common feature—reverence for 'the high ground'.

We know this because the people of The Lakes (exemplified by the people of Heaning Wood) and the people of Star Carr were both ultimately affected when 'Doggerland' in the east finally sunk beneath the waves of the North Sea.

The sinking of Doggerland in the east drove the people of Doggerland who were closest to Starcarria, westwards into Starcarria, which in turn drove some of the people of Starcarria further westwards, who took refuge in the high ground of The Lakes—not just because they needed to travel westwards, but because 'the rising of the tide' gave them reverence for "the high ground", wherever it was: those who came westwards merely bumped into the highlands of The Lakes!

As we shall soon see, this was the broad mechanics of how the heritage of Star Carr was introduced to The Lakes, which, over several thousand years, descended to the Carvetii, then to the people of Rheged, then to the people of Cumberland.

To put this into context, the sea level during the last ice age was much lower than today—indeed, the North Sea did not exist, and its water was restricted to a small region off the coast of Norway, now known as the Norwegian Trench.

This whole matter joined Britain to both mainland Europe and Scandinavia. It was a vast land whose lowlands slowly sank into the sea as the glaciers of the last ice age slowly melted, progressively raising the sea

87

level.

We remember the land eastwards of modern Britain as "Doggerland", but now, 12,000 years later, after the melt of the ice age caused Doggerland to sink beneath the waves as the sea level progressively rose, it can be seen on many maps as the Dogger Bank fishing grounds.

Dogger Bank was Doggerland's high ground, and it is directly eastwards of Star Carr—Doggerland goes out towards Norway and Denmark to the east, and Poland, Germany, Belgium, and the Netherlands to the south-east, with Dogger Bank being closest to Britain's east coast—and the coast of Starcarria, at that!

Yet, with Doggerland having now sunken beneath the North Sea, it is obvious that the people of Doggerland would have seen what we now call Great Britain as Doggerland's western highlands and Doggerland as its eastern lowlands.

The people of Britain and the people of Doggerland's highlands were, in essence, the very same people who were spread over a broader area that went at least to the high ground of Dogger Bank, and this means that we are now a people who once belonged to a place much larger than our modern self, who—having been subject to The Great Flood of adversity that came upon us in ancient times—became so tenacious in the face of adversity that closer to modern times we started identifying as 'ravens who would always get from one side of adversity to the other'.

Just like The Great Flood is recorded in the Book of Genesis as part of the origin story of the Jewish nation, we Celts of Britain have our own Great Flood origin story!

The Four Great Prophecies of Arthurian Britain

Significantly, just like the scribes of the Old World who wrote the Book of Genesis used the Old World symbol of the raven to identify the promise of getting from one side of adversity to the other, we Celts of Britain adopted that symbol as our own, doing so with such tenacity that even the people of the most central Celtic nation in Britain—the people of **Rheged**, a.k.a. **Cumberland**—identified themselves as Ravens of Rheged.

Curiously, three of "The Four Great Prophecies of Arthurian Britain" mention ravens!

The Four Great Prophecies of Arthurian Britain are the following:

1. So long as the Head of Bran faces south on Britain's White Mount, Britain will be protected. 1st Century. (n.b. "Bran" means raven.)

90

2. Arthur will return as a raven. Post-'Age of Arthur'. (n.b. "arth" means bear.)
3. The Red Dragon will be temporarily wounded by The White Dragon, but then The Red Dragon will rise and kill The White Dragon. Post-'Age of Arthur'.
4. So long as there are ravens in the Tower of London, England will be protected. Post-1066, an evolution of the previous 1st-century Prophecy of Bran.

At face value, these prophecies all seem to concern the struggle between the indigenous Britons of this land and its invaders; however, common to all of them is the notion of getting from one side of adversity to the other: they were all promises—even the last one, which states, "*So long as*...".

In the last one, the ravens can be seen as if symbolically "chained" to The Tower of London!

This 'chaining' can be seen to be a result of the Kingdom of Rheged having been joined to the Anglo-Saxons in that dynastic marriage between Rhiainfellt, Queen of Rheged, and Oswiu, who became the 7th Anglo-Saxon High King: so long as the Ravens of Rheged were in allegiance with the Anglo-Saxons, England would be protected!

To control Rheged was to control the centre of mainland Britain, which was to control Britain itself!

Whereas the Ravens of Rheged had the natural tendency to overcome all of adversity—because "a raven will do what ravens do"—we would have ordinarily expected the 'Ravens' of Rheged to eventually expel the Anglo-Saxons from Britain!

Yet the very nature of the dynastic marriage between Rhiainfellt and Oswiu not only prevented them from doing so, but it ironically made them the guarantor of the Anglo-Saxons' longevity in Britain!

Naturally, the "**So long as** ..." caveat in that prophecy was a promise that the ravens would eventually be 're-leased from The Tower'.

It should also be realised that the prophecy about 'the ravens in The Tower' has to be interpreted as being consistent with the other three prophecies, and these indicate that the ravens will prevail over Anglo-Saxon Britain in the long term, anyway!

But that is a story for another day, which I plan to be Book #3 in this *Raven Lore Children's Series,* "The Secret Cypher of Why There Are Ravens in the Tower of London".

Of course, it was the symbol of the Red Dragon in the third prophecy that Arthur represented when he valiantly fought the Anglo-Saxons—and as we know, Arthur is still to "return as a raven", as promised in the second prophecy!

The Minutiae of our own Great Flood

Between 10,000 BC and 6,170 BC, the ice of the last ice age progressively melted, and this caused the sea level to slowly rise. The rising of the sea not only caused Doggerland to sink beneath the sea, but it also caused our own coastlines to recede as well.

At the time of Heaning Man and Star Carr, around 9,000 BC, the eastern coast of Britain adjacent to Star Carr could have been further than sixty miles eastward of where it is today—the distance of the present day east coast of Britain to Dogger Bank is sixty miles—and the western coast adjacent to Heaning Wood, near Ulverston, would have been at least 80 miles further westward, reaching out beyond the Isle of Man.

During that period, the people of

Heaning Wood could have walked in a direct line to Anglesey, then in a direct line between Anglesey and the Isle of Man, then in a direct line to Scotland, then in a direct line back to Heaning Wood!

It is curious to think that when one now stands on the Cumberland coast at Whitehaven—which was once Great Britain's third busiest sea port—the same westwards gaze to the Isle of Man during Heaning Man's time would have looked over the verdant green lowlands between Whitehaven and Man, which we indigenous folk now call the Cumberland Basin.

Can you imagine looking westwards from 'the highlands' of Whitehaven during that period, seeing the distant trails of rising blue smoke of early morning cooking fires rising above plush verdant forests, with the occasional cerulean blue lake dispersed here and there between them? Even The Lake District extended much further westwards!

Of course, anyone cooking at those distant fires, looking eastwards towards the rising sun from those 'lowlands of the Cumberland Basin', would have seen Whitehaven as part of these western highlands of Britain!

The curious thing about the west coast of Cumberland is that it is directly westwards of the henge King Arthur's Round Table, illustrating that it is now the centre-most western coast of mainland Great Britain.

This gradual 'rising of the tide', which eventually swallowed the lowlands of the Cumberland Basin, illustrates that its now risen waters were always a contiguous part of mainland Britain.

In that sense, these waters are not really part of 'The Irish Sea', but instead, are part of a **bight** of the contiguous mainland of Great Britain.

A bight is a bend or curve in a shoreline, and examples of well-known bights include the following four:

1. The Bay of Biscay in Europe, which is larger than this bight but is a similar shape;
2. Hudson Bay in Canada, which has islands as 'pillars' at its entrance in a similar sense that this bight has Anglesey and the Isle of Man standing as pillars to guard its entrance;
3. The Great Australian Bight in Australia, which at its smallest calculation is 720 miles long; and,
4. The Southern California Bight is a 430-mile-long, curved stretch of coastline in the Americas that runs from California to Mexico.

What would be a good name for this bight?

Although we can readily identify the now sunken lowlands as the Cumberland Basin—similar to how we identify the now sunken Doggerland as Dogger Bank in the east—it's hardly a good name for a bight when a better one is easily supported by the bard Taliesin in the sixth Century:

"Darogan Myrddin dyfed breienin
O Gymru wherein o gambwri;
Dywawd derwyddon dadenci balon
O bil eryron o Eryron."

Geoffrey of Monmouth translated this in the 12th Century:

"Merlin prophesied that a king would come
From amongst the Welsh by heroism;
Druids foretold of the birth of noblemen
From the lineage of the lords of Eryri."

Taliesin was the chief bard at the court of Urien, King of Rheged. He probably composed this at the fort of Caer Luel—modern-day Carlisle— one of Urien's chief strongholds.

The subtlety of the translation "lords of Eryri"—lords of the Land of Eagles—is that it identifies a land that can broadly be described as all of that land and sea within a 50-mile range of Armboth, which is located on the western shore of Thirlmere, the middle lake of The Lake District.

These discoveries were recently made because of advances in the science of etymology over the last twenty years.

Although we shall, for now, leave this translation as "Land of Eagles", I should point out that back at the foot of Page 32, I gave the example of the Old Welsh kenning:

• The kenning *Eryr y mynydd* translates as "eagle of the mountain" to mean "powerful or majestic warrior".

So although we have rightly translated Taliesin's original 'eryron o Eryron' through Monmouth's "Lords of Eryri" to identify a *Land of Eagles,* we also have to contend that one of the reasons that this land was so precious to Urien, King of Rheged, was that the symbol of the eagles represented a kenning, perhaps "Land of Most Powerful", or something of that ilk.

I thoroughly explain the mechanics that prove that the western coast of Cumberland is in the "Land of Eagles" in my book *The Secret Cypher of Chalice Well*.

Broadly, it is based upon proving that Armboth was the central breeding ground of this 'Land of Eagles'.

The rationale behind how far it extends is that any eagle within a 50-mile radius of Armboth would have been able to see Golden Eagles soaring over Armboth during the breeding season, doing so with their feathered friends the Sea Eagle and White-Tailed Eagle.

My book *The Secret Cypher of Chalice Well* also explains how Armboth is proven to be the centre of the breeding grounds of all three of these eagle species in the district.

This proof includes the support of Taliesin and Aneirin, both 6th-century bards of the Court of Urien, King of Rheged!

The strict definition of this "Land of Eagles" is as far as an eagle could see from Armboth on a clear day, which radius falls just three miles short of the Isle of Man. Therefore, it would be reasonable to name the whole bight the "Bight of Eagles".

The significance of using this naming convention is that it was just as true during Taliesin's age of the Sixth Century as during the age of Heaning Man and Star Carr—that bight-curvature existed *somewhere* westward.

Heaning Man was also located in this "Land of Eagles", who would have understood the meaning of this name in his own language.

The reason that this is relevant comes down to the realisation that the rising sea levels during the period of 10,000 to 6,170 BC also corresponds with both of Britain's *western* and *eastern* coastlines progressively retreating during that same period—and that would have put pressure on both existing *western* **and** *eastern* populations to also progressively retreat towards the highlands of Central Britain that we are familiar with today.

Naturally, Doggerland and its associated Dogger Bank tend to get much more scientific and media interest than the Cumberland Basin, and that is because Doggerland is also relevant to Scandinavia and much of northern Europe.

However, just as Dogger Bank is to the east coast of Britain, the Cumberland Basin is to the west coast of Britain.

Both were flooded during the same period, and the flooding caused people on both sides of what is now mainland Great Britain to migrate to "the higher ground".

Naturally, this raises the question: "When is the scientific community going to give the same scrutiny to the former inhabitants of the settlements in the now-submerged Cumberland Basin as they do for the now-submerged Dogger Bank and Doggerland?"

On the western side, the progressive flooding of the Cumberland Basin drove Heaning Man's contemporaries and their descendants progressively eastwards to "the high ground" of the County of Cumberland, as it is today.

On the eastern coast, the progressive flooding of Doggerland drove the contemporaries of The Stag People of Star Carr progressively westward.

On the map on Page 83, you'll have noticed that I have broadly defined the west-to-east regions from the Cumberland Coast to the Star Carr Coast as **Carria**, **Mesocarria**, and **Starcarria**, respectively.

Although the etymology of Star Carr is unknown, these names have reverence for 'Carria' being seen to derive from the Brittonic word "carv", which means stag or deer; this word is later attributed to the name of the tribe of the Carvetii—The Stag People—as the people of the central west of Britain were known to the Romans.

As such—given this history and the matter that the same circumstances applied—it is reasonable to attribute this same name of Carvetii backwards towards 9,000 BC, but de-Latinising it as Carria, in the process.

The name Mesocarria has the same root but with meso meaning middle.

The name Starcarria is a happy co-incidence with the name Star Carr, which has reverence for carria deriving from the Brittonic 'carv' being an ellipse to The Stag People of Star Carr—but with star deriving from the Brittonic 'staer', which means stair, so that together they mean "The Rising of The Stag"—yet another kenning!

Indeed, the curious thing about the name Star Carr being seen as though deriving from 'staer-carv' is that the earliest carpentry of Europe discovered at Star Carr was an elevated wooden platform that rose as a stair, or stage, upon which the rituals that involved the 21 Stag Headdresses were undertaken.

Furthermore—in the context of the 21 Stag Headdresses found at Star Carr representing the birth of stag-like social structures in Britain—the name Star Carr, having the idiom "The Rising of The Stag", is very significant indeed!

All of these naming conventions consider the proof that all three regions were subject to common forced migration patterns, which, in turn, allows us to make common suppositions about all of the people that we know who existed in all three of these regions, who can commonly be called "Stag People" from around 9,000 BC onwards.

The curious matter of fact is that Britain's own "Great Flood" origin story starts with the progressive "rising of the tide" over thousands of years, consistently pressing the people on both coasts to have reverence for 'The High Ground'.

Yet was this 'progressive retreat of both shorelines' enough for them to reach a tipping point where they consciously chose to identify as 'ravens' to illustrate that they always got from one side of adversity to another? Perhaps not.

But around 6,170 BC, an event of such a tragic magnitude became Britain's clear tipping point. From that time, the survivors had a clear reason to not only have a deep reverence for 'the high ground' but also—as the survivors of a tragic event that was of such magnitude that nothing worse could have happened to them—they resolved to always "get from one side of any adversity to the other, where 'the dove of peace could be released'". Their motto was essentially, "We will survive, revere the high ground!"

Naturally, it is unknown when the old world symbols of the raven and dove were first attributed to be symbols having those meanings that we understand today, but it's clear that when the old world had developed so far as to attribute these symbols as stated, that the people of central Britain were already predisposed to accept them as badges of honour.

If 'Barney Rubble and Fred Flintstone' were prehistoric Britons, you could imagine their conversation, "If that is what a 'raven' is, then we is what a 'raven' is!"—eventually leading to not just the self-identification of "The Ravens of Rheged" in later centuries, but also to native Britons at large seeing themselves as 'ravens', a phenomenon that they eventually shared with the continental Celts!

The tragic event that became this tipping point was the greatest submarine landslide that the world has ever known. This caused a tsunami of such magnitude that all of the remnants of Doggerland at the time of the tsunami were completely devastated. That tsunami is even thought to have opened the North Sea to the English Channel!

This submarine event is known as the "Storegga Slide". It originated off the coast of Norway, just north of the body of water known as the Norwegian Trench.

This happened around 6,170 BC, and it is poignant to note that when it happened, not only was Britain's whole eastern coast devastated by the tsunami, but those people who were involved in the devastation and who survived already had a known history of the waters progressively rising to threaten them over the thousands of years that preceded them.

The Storegga Slide was the prehistoric Briton "I told you so!" event.

During the age of Heaning Man and Star Carr, their own recent memory was already one of "The Great Ice Wall In The North" progressively melting.

Between then and the devastation that the Storegga Slide caused, the relentless pressure of both Doggerland and the Cumberland Basin being progressively drowned had already forced the people of our own prehistoric highlands to become a resilient people.

The fact that the Storegga Slide was most devastating to the eastern coast also affected how the peoples of both East and West continued to develop—there was, in time, a noticeable divergence between them!

On the one hand, the rising tide caused a substantial migration from Doggerland in the far east into Starcarria in the near east, and the 'flood of people' from Doggerland upon the people of Starcarria would have caused many of the existing people of Starcarria to migrate westwards—with many of them ultimately reaching the highlands of The Lakes in the west.

Yet those refugees who had reached Starcarria from Doggerland would have typically been content to put down roots in Starcarria itself, who would have been less inclined to continue migrating westwards.

Why would they prolong the adversity of their westwards odyssey when having reached 'the promised land of Starcarria', they could settle with the rest of the people of Doggerland who had come with them?

The tragedy was one thing, but why would they want to disperse further when they could settle in the comfort of their existing Dogger communities?

Yet to those existing natives of Starcarria—who were already familiar with 'the rising tide' of their own eastern coast—then migrating west was their best chance to preserve their own community as "The Stag People"—who, having migrated westwards, became known as the Carvetii several thousand years later.

By these same tokens, the 'Dogger-come-Star Carr' brotherhood would later mix with those in Mesocarria to become the northern part of the Celtic tribe called the Brigantes, and because the Proto-Celtic root of their name, *brigant-, means "high, elevated", there has been some very strong supposition that such of their settlements like Brigantium were so-named as "High Ones" to represent the metaphorical sense of nobility, or perhaps just represent the 'highlands' of the Pennines.

Both options could be traced back, at least as far as the Storegga Slide that destroyed Doggerland.

On the one hand, the combined descendants of Star Carr and Dogger's refugees may have descended the ages with reverence for the image of those 21 Stag Headdresses representing the apex of their social structure as 'risen stags'—hence attributing their people with the notion of being "High People" in the sense of nobility.

On the other hand, the trauma of the tsunami that destroyed Doggerland may have descended to give them a reverence for 'the highlands'.

A third option is most likely, and that is with both notions continuing to be revered under the concept of the people themselves being 'The High People' for both of these reasons.

This opinion is easily fortified by the matter that reverence in the West for those original symbols of Stag Head-dresses descended in people who become known as the Carvetii.

Yet those in the west were not entangled with the grief of the loss of Doggerland, and that's because those western peoples predominantly consisted of the contraction westwards of the original peoples of Starcarria combining with the peoples of the eastwards contraction of the Cumberland Basin.

Here, the divergence between west and east resulted from the refugees from Doggerland primarily staying in the east in Starcarria after the Storegga Slide!

To understand how the Brigantes became so significant in the east, it is worthwhile considering the adversity that the common people of Starcarria and Doggerland endured over the ages that Doggerland sank.

Was there ever a distinction between the high ground of Doggerland and the east of Britain during that age?

Although Doggerland covered the full extent of the North Sea, extending to mainland Europe in the south and southeast and to Scandinavia in the east and northeast, the high grounds of Dogger Bank were very close to what we now regard as mainland Great Britain—just 60 miles away!

Those highlands of Doggerland that

we now remember as the fishing grounds of Dogger Bank were so close to mainland Great Britain that the rest of the people of Doggerland would have likely seen the highlands of Dogger Bank as merely part of the western highlands of Britain to their west!

Here in Britain, we'd have probably considered that 'the lowlands of Dog-gerland' started eastwards of Dog-ger Bank, claiming those highlands to be part of our own 'highlands' of that age.

This is why I stated much earlier, that:

- We are now a people who once belonged to a place much larger than our modern self, who—having been subject to The Great Flood of adversity that came upon us in an-cient times—became so tenacious in the face of adversity that closer to modern times we started identi-fying as 'ravens who would always get from one side of adversity to the other'.

To get a better understanding of how Doggerland progressively sank, I've broken down its transition from being wholly above sea level to fully submerged, as follows:

1. **Initial Formation of Doggerland**: Doggerland was originally a large area of land that connected what is now the British Isles to mainland Europe and Scandinavia during periods of lower sea levels. This landmass was above water during the last glacial maximum, which occurred approximately 20,000 years ago when much of the Earth's water was locked up in ice sheets.

2. **Rising Sea Levels**: As the Earth's climate warmed and the ice sheets began to melt, sea levels began to rise. This gradual rise would have started submerging Doggerland's low-lying areas.

3. **Formation of Islands**: As sea levels continued to rise, higher elevations within Doggerland would have become islands. These islands formed due to the persistence of higher ground that remained above water.

4. **Archipelago Formation**: Over time, as sea levels continued to rise, the higher-elevation islands may have fragmented into smaller landmasses, forming an archipelago. Erosion and the submersion of lower-lying areas played a role in this fragmentation.

5. **Continued Sea-Level Rise:** Sea levels continued to rise over thousands of years, and the archipelago's landmasses, including the islands, would have gradually shrunk. This process would have been influenced by factors such as the sea-level rise rate and the land's geological composition.

6. **Submergence of Doggerland**: As sea levels continued to rise, the remaining landmasses, including the

archipelago, would have eventually been completely submerged beneath the sea. This submersion marked the end of Doggerland as a recognisable landmass.

7. **Formation of Dogger Bank**: Dogger Bank is a large underwater sandbank located in the North Sea today. It likely formed from sediment deposition over thousands of years after the complete submergence of Doggerland. This sediment accumulation created the shallow underwater feature known as Dogger Bank, presumed to represent the original high ground of Doggerland but as now being covered in a veneer of that sediment.

A survey of the seabed also leads us to believe that in the three hundred years of the growing flooding of Dogger Island that preceded that tsunami of 6,170 BC, when the sea level naturally rose in that age before that inevitable catastrophe, an exodus of refugees from Dogger Island would have caused a significant westward migration into Great Britain by those who were progressively escaping the rising sea-levels around Dogger Island as it progressively sunk to become the Dogger Archipelago.

During this period of Doggerland's drowning, the closest coast to the Dogger Island highland of Doggerland was the eastern coast of Starcarria—making it the most likely target of Doggerland's remaining refugees: they just needed to follow the setting sun!

Curiously, those last remaining high grounds of Dogger Island can be seen underwater as Dogger Bank and its surrounding shelf, which is about the same size as Cumbria from its north to south—or a little more.

To make matters worse, the north of Dogger Island was directly eastwards of the north of Cumbria, making landfall between them on today's east coast around Sunderland; and the south of Dogger Island was directly eastwards of the south of Cumbria, making landfall between them around 20 miles south of where Star Carr is located.

This means that towards the end of Doggerland's existence as Dogger Island, the significant westward migration of the people of Dogger Island into Starcarria—combined with the matter that Dogger Island had been the same size as Starcarria-—would mean that substantial inward refugee numbers from Dogger Island into Starcarria would have been disruptive to the people of Star Carr.

They'd have been overrun by perhaps one inbound refugee for every existing resident.

This presumes that the populations between Dogger Island and Cumbria on those shared eastings were initially evenly distributed before the flooding of Doggerland gradually increased to transform it into Dogger Island.

This, in turn, would mean that when those refugees started migrating westwards in their boats to the coast of Britain to avoid the growing certainty of Dogger Island completely sinking, that the region around Star Carr, and northwards of it—which we are calling "Starcarria"—would have potentially been overrun by the migration of a population into it that was equivalent to the size of the existing population of Starcarria in the east—but also equivalent to the existing equally-sized population of Cumbria, in the west.

This would have caused some of those who we know were already living in the region of Star Carr to migrate westwards towards the now familiar territories of The Lakes.

We should also remember that the

migration of refugees from Dogger Island was not the only pressure on the people of Starcarria.

This is because the rising sea level that was causing Dogger Island to sink was also causing the east coast of Starcarria to contract westwards.

So, not only did the people of Starcarria have to put up with refugees from Doggerland coming westwards to them, but they also had to put up with the pressure of their own people having to move westwards from the vicinity of the coast, as the coast itself receded westwards.

In short, the common catch-cry of Dogger Island and Starcarria was "Tally-ho, westwards ho!"—in both cases, the message was simple: 'Value the high ground!'

The big picture that I've tried to paint here is that there was once a common region that extended from modern-day Cumbria in the west across to the corresponding eastern coast on the same latitudes, which eventually divided into two, Cumbria in the west and Starcarria in the east, with a median-strip in the middle between them, with those in the west eventually becoming the Carvetii.

Naturally, rather than calling the west by the name of 'Cumbria'—which is a post-1974 *administrative* axiom in this region which until 1974 **ONLY** applied to Cumberland—let's call the same region in the time we refer to Starcarria as being "Carria" (also from the 'carv' in Carvetii, meaning stag), thus shortened to Carria.

The 'Ascent' of Arthurian Britain

Although we generally hold that the Age of Arthur was between 350 and 650 AD—with Arthur himself having lived from perhaps late in the 5th Century to around 537 AD, dying at the Battle of Camlann—the **ascent** of

Arthurian Britain can be seen traversing every age from the melt of the last ice age around 12,000 years ago, and although becoming focal during the Age of Arthur, continuing past that age, right up to the present day.

The peculiarity about the Four Great Prophecies of Arthurian Britain is that all four are strictly committed to always getting from one side of adversity to the other—no matter how long it takes—so the ascent of Arthurian Britain can be said to always subsist in 'The Present', with The Present forever continuing to leave its footprints in the past.

Today's footprint inevitably becomes yesterday's!

This matter is perhaps best represented in the **Crux of Arthurian Canon**—the prophecy that "Arthur will return as a raven"—because, indeed, we don't know how many times Arthur has already returned as a raven in the past, nor how many times he will need to do so in the future!

Who is to say that in 55 and 54 BC, when Julius Caesar tried to invade Britain, that our ancient Briton ancestors were not already saying, "We will stand our ground as a bear would, defending our territory, even to the death!"—who, in doing so, hailed their leader as "The Bear" using some sort of lingual construct that would later evolve into the Old Welsh "Arthur" where **arth** means bear?

This would illustrate why the Welsh have never adopted a regnal number—that number was probably unknown at any time!

Although we tend to regard the Arthurian fabric as Celtic, our even more ancient folk may have had similar notions before we adapted to the new emerging theocracy of the age—the introduction of Celticity to our ancient forebears, who, after three generations of having adopted it, became Celtic.

Perhaps even our Celticity is a veneer upon our more ancient "Arthurian" self!

Here, the pertinent questions are:

1. When did our ancient ancestors start adopting familiar Arthurian imagery like 'The Bear' returning as a 'Raven'?
2. Were we already Celtic when we adopted this familiar imagery, or had we already assimilated this imagery by the time we became Celtic?

Our own "Great Flood" origin story of The Flood of Doggerland had already made us resilient by the aftermath of that tragedy in 6,170 BC.

As the survivors of the tragic event of the Storegga Slide—which was of such magnitude that nothing worse could have happened to us—we had clearly resolved to always "get from one side of any adversity to the other so that 'the dove of peace could be released'"—we'd have adopted this resolution by around 6,000 BC.

So that accommodates the "Raven" component of the Crux of Arthurian Canon—the capacity to always get from one side of adversity to the other—but when did our nature of "standing our ground as a 'bear' would" become so ingrained into our nature that both 'bear and raven' complemented each other—doing it so well as to bond into a mutually connected part of our consciousness as that now familiar prophecy?

Clearly, this had to be before the henge was built—the formality of "The Leaders of Britain meeting at a central meeting place to exchange **oaths** amongst one and another" expresses that "these **oaths** are to be *defended* as being right and true".

That is, those leaders who made oaths at the henge were compelled to defend them 'as a bear would'—and this is what made the henge "Arthur's Round Table".

By the time the henge was built, the nature of 'Arth', which means bear, had become a concept that related to the nature where we stood our ground.

Naturally, we don't know if we were already Celtic when the henge was built; on the one hand, the traditional doctrine of the last three hundred years has been that we became Celtic in Britain around seven or eight hundred BC—which is well after the henge was built!

However, Cunliffe and Koch's "Celtic from the West" theory supposes that we might have become Celtic much earlier than traditionally thought.

Cunliffe has more recently proposed

that Proto-Celtic could have been established as early as 3,000 BC.

This might suggest that we were Proto-Celtic up until a few hundred years before the henge was built, but that the building of the henge represented our actual transition from being Proto-Celtic to being Celtic.

If so, that would give the henge the likely origin story that this "central meeting place" was needed to accommodate how tribes of uniform "Celticity" were needing to uniformly engage with each other despite being dispersed right across the land.

Perhaps our 'stag-like' social structures became even better formulated because the rigours of Celticity provided better communication structures that tended to express common notions more uniformly!

However, whether Celtic or not, we can say that by the time the henge was built, we had already become "Arthurian"—that is, we were already committed to transcending any adversity that came upon us, as well as "standing the ground of the oaths that we had taken at the henge".

Whether or not we associated these characteristics using the respective symbols of raven and bear by the time the henge was built is not easily determined—but we can say that this **nature** was already *characterised* as *being* **imbued** *within us* by then!

Similarly, by having already adopted reverence for stag-like social structures as early as 9,000 BC, the Carvetii had probably found it relatively easy to adopt that underlying nature as their name—The Stag People—and by the time that Nicene Christianity was declared as the official state religion of the Roman Empire in 380 AD, imagery of stags were becoming Christian-like, having easily been drawn from nine thousand years of 'stag-like' prehistory.

Naturally, the ascent of Arthurian Britain also includes those various Arthurian Cycles that we are familiar with—but here's the crux: "From which parts of our prehistory were those images drawn?"

For example, the most widely distributed neolithic stone axes, and other such cutting implements, are known to have come from the Langdale Axe Factories in the heart of the Lake District, just four miles south of the central lake, Thirlmere.

On the one hand, the "double-edged sword of truth" that we know as Excalibur can be easily seen to have been drawn from 'Langdale' stone—and I mean this in the figurative sense that even just the concept of 'the double-edged sword of truth' had to have its origin in notions that were rooted in ancient deep-seated experiences that revolve around an understanding of what "a cutting edge" is.

Without having a history of cutting implements, the notion "the double-edged sword of truth" could not have been coined!

Because of that, it's rather easy to realise that the neolithic evolution of cutting implements that are symbolised by the name "Langdale" stone— under that notion because it was the leading 'brand'—was a contributory part of Arthurian prehistory!

In this sense, everything from Arthurian prehistory that eventually contributed to Arthurian imagery can be described as Proto-Arthurian.

Hence, the Proto-Arthurian period goes back to at least the image of The Leftwards Facing Stag at Creswell Crags, c. 10,500 BC. And because the 'ascent' of Arthurian Britain *includes* its 'Proto' Arthurian stage, then it is quite reasonable to characterise "The Ascent of Arthurian Britain" as having started at least 12,500 years ago!

Furthermore, the matter that the Ascent of Arthurian Britain can also be said to always subsist in the present—with 'the present' characteristically moving forward, step by step, day by day—then "The Soil" in which the Great Arthurian Forrest is rooted in has to be said to be everything in the last 12,500 years of British history that can be attributed to having contributed to the "ascent" of Arthurian Britain.

How would you define Arthurian Britain?

Here are three prevailing root contexts, from which *every* Arthurian cycle has flowered and flourished:

- "**Arthurian Britain**": The nature of Britons to stand their ground 'as a bear' would, with the tenacity to fight to survive any adversity as a raven would.

- **"Arthurian Briton"**: an indigenous Briton who stands their ground 'as a bear' would, with the tenacity to fight to survive any adversity as a raven would.

- **"Arthurian British"**: someone who has the right of residency in Britain, but without having yet naturalised as a Briton has the right to call themselves British by virtue of that right of residency, who stands the ground of the Britons in solidarity with them 'as a bear' would, with the tenacity to fight to survive any adversity as a raven would.

You will notice that I have reverence for the proper use of the suffix '-ish', which the Cambridge Dictionary expounds as follows:

-ish suffix—used to form *adjectives* to give the meaning *to some degree*. (Italics mine)

134

Given the proper use of that suffix, I offer the following four examples.

Although I acknowledge that some people with nationalistic tendencies might not presently agree with the whole scope of these definitions, I am confident that they will become more widely accepted the closer we get to "Arthur once again drawing the double-edged sword of truth from the stone".

I offer these four definitions, as follows:

1. **English**: describes someone with a mere right of residency in England, who, without having naturalised as an Anglo-Saxon is **articulated** to the Anglo-Saxons by that right of residency, hence is Engl**ish**.
2. **Scottish**: describes someone with a mere right of residency in Scotland, who, without having naturalised as a Scoti is **articulated** to the Scoti by that right of residency,

hence is Scott**ish**.

3. **Welshish**: describes someone with a mere right of residency in Wales, who, without having naturalised as Welsh is **articulated** to the Welsh by that right of residency, hence is Welsh**ish**—more often expressed as Welshy.

4. **British**: describes someone with a mere right of residency in Britain, who, without having naturalised as a Briton, is **articulated** to the Britons by that right of residency, hence is Brit**ish**.

Having reverence for these meanings is a good step down the road towards "Arthur drawing the double-edged sword of truth from the stone"—*use the truth to become it!*

The Great Arthurian Forrest

Sometime in the distant Arthurian past, our Brythonic ancestors developed a communication method called **Awen**.

Awen can be described as "a poetic breeze of inspiration that causes **meanings** to rise as if they were 'eagles of evangelism' soaring on a rising breeze"—and this is meant in the sense that these poetic 'eagles of evangelism' fly so high as being imbued with truths that would otherwise be quite complex to say yet are simultaneously distributed as though the wider meaning is conveyed 'evangelically'; that is, the broader complex meaning is conveyed 'on the wings of the eagles'—in one sense they can be described as kennings—and yet in another sense, they can be described as circumlocutions where *the recipient* of the communication *infers their intended meaning*, instead of the sender actually stating it!

This goes well beyond awen merely being an expression of "poetic inspiration, muse"—which is its broad *clinical*, dictionary definition—and instead ventures into a world where all three of this land's **history**, its ancient **prophecies**, and its **destiny** are interleaved; it is one thing to say that something is a metaphor, but when it is called awen, it is also attached to the tongues of our ancient prophets!

Someone who expresses awen is an Awenydd—this is pronounced A-wen-ith in English where the 'th' is voiced like the 'th' in 'this'—and when an Awenydd speaks, you hear not just his tongue but the chorus of all the tongues of our ancient bards as well.

The uninitiated may hear a particular composition's modern-day author talking. Yet, those familiar with awen will also hear other bards, such as Taliesin and Aneirin, speaking from the 6th century.

One of the universal examples that Awenydds typically present to Students of Awen is Taliesin's 6th-century expression of it in the following lines:

ban pan doeth peir
ogyrwen awen teir

Although this explicitly means "the three elements of inspiration that came, splendid, out of the cauldron", it implicitly means "... inspiration that came from God" because 'peir', which can mean cauldron, can also mean sovereign with the meaning of "God".

This is a perfect example of a kenning being used as a circumlocution. - It is up to the recipient of the verse to infer its meaning; yet what tools does the recipient have to determine which meaning he will select to infer?

The answer is clear: the listener has all of the Brythonic Awen available to him as a tool to guide his decisions, upon which he should listen to the tongues of every bard and prophet that has been before him.

The beauty of awen is that all of Brythonic Awen is interleaved—for example, consider the following!

Elider Sais, writing in the 13th century, in 'singing to Christ' wrote:

'Brilliant my poetry after Myrddin
Shining forth from the cauldron of awen'

Of course, the 'dd' in Myrddin is also pronounced as a voiced 'th' as before, and here, Elider Sais was effectively saying that his poetry, written in the ilk of those familiar speech patterns usually attributed to the bard Merlin, 'shone forth from the very heart of God' and thus in itself should be seen as having been intended to be accepted as a holy expression.

Because Taliesin associates the word *awen* with the Celtic word *peir*, then when you see Celtic drawings depicting a cauldron, you should think, "What's the awen here?" instead of dismissing it as something from a bygone age as if thinking, "What brutish pagan devilry was going on there?"

In this sense, but using what might be described as a 21st-century metaphor, Celtic awen can be allegorised as if preordained to convey various ideals as though they were 'packaged in an envelope'.

For example, consider an envelope that is engraved on the outside with the expression "Arthur will return as a raven".

1. You will already understand the meaning of this expression, because in this book you've already studied the Celtic symbols.
2. Yet explaining this meaning to a novice might take thousands of words before you could be sure that he understood it.
3. It is as though the expression of Awen is what is engraved on the outside of the envelope, and the

thousands of words that you'd need to explain its meaning are the words that you put inside the envelope.

4. Awenydds already understand the expression, so they do not need to look inside the envelope.

5. Historically, children are taught the meanings of these expressions as they grow up.

6. Children who have been taught these meanings thus have learned to understand them, so they also do not need to look inside the envelope.

7. This illustrates how simple Expressions of Awen are passed from generation to generation to convey complex ideas from one generation to the next.

Similarly, it is like saying, "A proverb is what is written on the outside of an envelope, and the lengths that you might go to explain the proverb is that which you'd put inside the envelope which carries it."

Awen is the Brythonic form in which truths are traditionally expressed to be passed on **compactly** *from generation to generation!*

It is from this 'Realm of Awen' that we get an understanding of what **The Great Arthurian Forrest** is—and it would not be improper to say that The Great Arthurian Forrest has its origin in The Cauldron of Awen itself.

Here, I'm merely dwelling on poetic licence by using that expression as an ellipse to the Brythonic word peir, which allows us to visualise a source of inspiration as a 'pool'—a collection of ideas in which visions of destiny can be seen!

On the one hand, we know that the historical Arthur fought to defend indigenous Britain from the onslaught of the Anglo-Saxons.

But on the other hand, we must ask, "What was Arthur and his army of

Britons fighting to protect?"

The clear answer to this question— communicated as an Expression of Awen—is that Arthur and our ancient ancestors were fighting to protect "The Great Arthurian Forrest" itself.

- What is this Great Arthurian Forrest?
- What complex ideas are vested in the imagery of this awen, designed to be handed down from generation to generation?

On the one hand, the name "The Great Arthurian Forrest" is an Expression of Awen. Yet on the other hand, here come all of the words that I'll need to explain it!

Where I've previously said that the **Ascent** of Arthurian Britain can be traced back 12,500 years but always subsists in "The Present"—forever taking discreet steps forward towards our future generations as though leaving footsteps in the soil that show from where we came—it is the answer to the question, "What is this Great Arthurian Forrest?" *that shows where we are going.*

For example, we often look at our own 'family tree' as though its root represents the genesis of our past—which, of course, is true.

However, it is the same family tree that will sprout the branches of the new generation and thus sprout *the generations of our future—**as such, it also represents the genesis of our future!***

Our family trees, like the legends of King Arthur, are not just relics of the past. They are the guardians of our future, standing firm and protecting it with the strength of a bear 'as if standing its ground to protect it' *as a bear would!*

In this sense, you should realise that

anything you can express as **awen** that represents 'standing the ground of your future' as an extension of our Arthurian past, *is fundamentally Arthurian.*

That is, just as *arth* ('the bear') stands to protect something "as a bear would"—because *bears will do what bears will do*—then the expression "The Great Arthurian Forrest" is a **Cypher of Awen** that compactly extols some very profound concepts that we Britons are predestined to pass from generation to generation, down through the ages.

Here, the stark headline is that where we see an expression that advertises something as being *Arthurian*, we should question, "What heritage does this expression imply that we should 'stand the ground to protect' so that it can be passed from generation to generation?"

Of course, when "Arthur returns as a

raven" and who in doing so will have drawn the double-edged sword of truth, then it will be the "raven" in him who 'flies back and forth' over these expressions, 'beating its wings so that anything false will be dried from it'—this will be the mechanism that chooses which expressions are genuine and hence would identify which heritages should continue to be brought forth to new generations!

Naturally, our Arthurian destiny can only be visualised in the wider context as being consistent with the Four Great Prophecies of Arthurian Britain—as already discussed—yet the 'Camelot' of what this specific phrase, "The Great Arthurian Forrest" means, is distinct and with purpose!

I went to very great lengths to expound the meaning of this in my book *The Secret Cypher of Chalice Well,* where I treated it as a Secret Cypher: if you want greater detail than the following, then I would recommend that you add that book to your reading list.

Here, I'll cherry-pick a few expressions and ideas from that book so we can paint the picture of this forrest, as we need!

First, it is no secret that our ancient druid ancestors were tasked with being the 'oral repositories' of all knowledge related to the kingdom they were attached to.

Julius Caesar told the whole world this in 52 BC!

However, the following definition of the word *druid* may surprise you!

- **druid**: noun, borrowed from French druide, from Old French, via Latin Druidae, from Gaulish *druwits,- from Proto-Celtic *druwits (literally "**oak-knower**"), from Proto-Indo-European *dóru ("tree") and *weyd-("to see").

The exciting thing about this etymology is that it also contains an **Expression of Awen**: it was the role of the druids to be the "**oak-knowers**" of the Great Arthurian Forrest!

The question, of course, is what does the circumlocution of being an "Oak Knower" actually mean?

It is as though our ancient ancestors foretold that one's share of the land upon which one stood was based upon one having acquired a standing where one's **family** was considered to have substantially become an 'Oaken Tree' of the Great Arthurian Forrest—our "Family Tree".

In Arthurian terms, an *Oaken Tree* is a family that has existed for nine generations. The family head presides over the 'branches of his family tree' that are at most nine generations deep and nine generations wide.

So, on the one hand, one's "share"

of the land was determined by one's "oaken pedigree"—hence, one did not have to save up and buy the land—its distribution of 'ownership' was based upon the societal equality of having a pedigree that was more than nine generations on Briton soil.

On the other hand, the Celtic nation's "destiny" was based upon every ninth-generation family head who led a family whose branches were at most nine generations wide and nine generations deep being qualified by that pedigree to sit in the kingdom's National Council.

These family heads were each called a **Pencenedl**, and the national council they all belonged to was the Celtic nation's 'House of Lords', so to speak.

The destiny of the Celtic nation was decided by the democratic vote of all of these family heads, who, as such, were each a lord "crowned by the cap of the acorn that had since grown to become his oaken family tree".

Here's a **statement of fact** from the Archaeologia Cambrensis, July 1860:

- "A person passed the ninth descent formed a new **pencenedl**, or head of a family. Every family was represented by its elder, and these elders from every family were delegates to the national council. The origin of this system is buried in the depths of antiquity, for it was found to be in existence at the early part of the tenth century...". (bold text decoration, mine.)

So, clearly, you can see that these Expressions of Awen are actual juxtapositions of Expressions of Reality!

This is the oaken "Great Arthurian Forrest" that Arthur originally rode into battle to protect; as "The Son of Prosperity"—an expression I thoroughly expound in the book *The Secret Cypher of Chalice Well*—he was riding into battle to preserve the "Camelot" of how we lived, the "Camelot" of how land was equally distributed by those who had a pedigree that proved their worth, and the "Camelot" of how we democratically administered ourselves.

I wish to dwell on the matter of how profound this is: the promise that is conveyed by The Four Great Prophecies of Arthurian Britain is that every single person in the land whose pedigree on Briton soil was greater than nine generations had the **birthright** to a 'free allocation of land' when they came of age.

1. According to the prophecies, this is our indigenous nation's future.
2. How far in the future is only a matter of time.
3. According to these prophecies, everyone in Britain should start seeking to determine who heads up their oaken family tree.

Who is your 'oaken family lord', your pencenedl? What is the 'oaken pedigree' under this oaken family lord, to the ninth descent?

Children nationwide should undertake personal homework projects to identify who this person is—and his pedigree to at least the ninth descent—just as already happens in some parts of Wales today: your family trees should be proud school projects that line the walls of your classrooms!

If it turns out that you have not been here long enough to qualify for a family **pencenedl**, you should discover which of your friends do have one, and draw close to them.

This is part of the Arthurian way, this is partially how family alliances are formed!

I'd encourage that you and your friends, having identified who all of your respective Pencenedls were, that you then have parties with your friends, where each family pencenedl is introduced to each other.

Can you imagine what you would be doing here?

You'd be helping to create local committees of a Celtic National Council!

These pencenedls—the collection of yours and all your friends' family heads—they would form the basis of this country's **Indigenous National Council**, country-wide.

And if you are not living in Britain, consider doing this anyway—there's nothing wrong with there being a Celtic revival on the world stage!

Children-power! Ka-pow!

Get all your 'Chief Kens' together—your pencenedls (the 'c' is pronounced as a 'k' and pen means *chief,*

154

head, lord)—and then encourage all of the adults to talk about the Arthurian dream!

I shan't go into the minutiae here, but even those who had been here for three generations—the minimum time it took to naturalise as a genuine indigenous Briton—had the right to free land, but in the form of a minimal self-sustaining farm or croft—which, for a family of four, is generally thought to be around five acres. Those who have been in a country for under three generations are still accommodated in the dream, but in the context that it takes three generations to naturalise as a native of that land.

- This is like an 'immigration tax' that sorts out the genuine from the free-loaders.
- It is also the mechanism that regulates how much land is available to distribute for free to those who are the natives of the land.

- The formula is this: after three generations, one qualifies for a minimal farm or croft; after nine generations, one qualifies for a free share as a 'freeman' of the land.

This is the way it used to be. It is for the politicians of the new age to determine which pathways into this have propriety and which do not!

In terms of 'Briton grandeur on the world stage', one can imagine that the fulfilment of these prophecies will trigger a new sense of political propriety worldwide.

I imagine that there will be a new age of 'Greta Thunbergs' campaigning that everyone who is native to a nation should be distributed their fair share of free land, by birthright.

Ironically, a nation living a self-sustaining lifestyle on a properly forested share of land that can raise food and firewood needs is the best model of living that best protects the environment.

In this sense, the 'Greta Thunbergs' of this world would have a valid platform on which to stand. I'm not criticising those campaigners of the present; I'm just presenting the pre-destined dream to them:

- Free land for natives by mere birthright equates to free planetary sustainability that is maximised for the masses!
- The number of people who this would benefit clearly dominate the electorate, making this an inevitable future!
- Those who are on their own sustainable plots of land don't need to draw on a nation's social security budget, nor a pension budget—which if fully implemented in Britain would remove an annual expenditure of approximately 450 billion pounds sterling from the annual budget—which would be

a saving of around four and a half *trillion pounds* sterling each decade!

- Added to that economic saving would be various savings from unnecessary scientific expenditure.
- This is because 'Carbon Sequestration' is maximised where natives live a self-sustaining lifestyle on the land, who generally only consume what the land produces, and that anything that they do consume—such as firewood, food, and waste—is both disposed of locally and regenerated locally.
- Where needed, the reforestation of part of a farm to enable firewood production, even enhances these outcomes!

So, when we talk about The Great Arthurian Forrest, we're not just talking about a bunch of trees. We're talking about how we used to live, with everyone having a fair share of land, and how we made decisions together as a community.

This is what Arthur fought to protect—our way of life and our democratic way of governing ourselves.

As an idealisation, The Great Arthurian Forrest is **foremost** over all forests, with the spelling of Forrest with a double-r instead of forest with a single-r, alluding to this nature!

The Prevailing Significance of "The Oak-Knowers"

Although "The Ascent of Arthurian Britain" leads us to the leading edge of the present day, where every 24 hours, the footprints of today become the footprints of yesterday, we must acknowledge the significance of where those footprints first began.

Naturally, we can quite easily acknowledge:

1. That the building of the henge *King Arthur's Round Table* represents an **epoch of formality** where

The Leadership of Britannia started taking oaths between one tribe and another that represented a shift towards the trend of unified cohesion;

2. That from this time we were **already** Arthurian on the basis that by wanting to build the henge in the first place, the Leadership of Britannia was already demonstrating that it was tending to collectively 'stand the ground of the henge to protect those oaths as a bear would'; and,

3. That we can even consider that this 'Already Arthurian Line across The Sands of Time' *already* existed when King Arthur's Round Table was built.

Pushed to its limits, this thought experiment rapidly changes from the question of:

• "What came first, the Chicken-of-Celticity or the Egg-of-Arthurianism?", to

- "What *hatched* first, the Chicken-of-Celticity or the Egg-of-Arthurianism?"

Which of the following is most significant?

- "The hatching of the egg", or
- "The birthing of the chicken".

It doesn't take long to realise that the **gestation** of Arthurianism was key to the survival of Celticity, and because of that, the mere existence of the Chicken-of-Celticity would not have been possible without the Egg-of-Arthurianism hatching.

To attribute this with a rock-solid sense of reality, let's start with the premise that "Druidry is Arthurian", surmising from this that it must have been adopted into the wider Celticity of Europe **from Britain**.

In his work *Commentarii de Bello Gallico (The Gallic Wars)*, Julius Caesar wrote about the Druids and their practices, and in Book VI, Chapter 13, he mentions the origin of Druidry.

Here's the relevant passage, translated into English:

- "It is thought that the discipline (of the Druids) was discovered in Britain and carried from there into Gaul, and now those who wish to gain a more accurate knowledge of that system generally proceed to Britain to learn it."

This passage indicates that Caesar believed that Druidic practices originated in Britain and then spread to Gaul—and, by implication, to wider Celtic climes!

Although Caesar wrote this around 52 BC during the later years of his campaigns in Gaul, it is because Druidism "stands the ground" of protecting "the knowledge of their kind" that it can be described as *Arthurian*—so on this basis, it can be said that "Arthurianism started in Britain".

Caesar supports this notion by going on to say the following about the druids:

- "They attend to public and private sacrifices, explain religious questions, and have great authority. A large number of young men flock to them for the sake of instruction, and they are in great honour among them. For they determine concerning almost all controversies, public and private; and if any crime has been committed, if murder has been perpetrated, if there be any dispute about an inheritance, or about boundaries, they decide it; they decree rewards and punishments; if any one, either in a private or public capacity, does not abide by their decision, they interdict him from the sacrifices. This among them is the most severe punishment. Those who have been thus interdicted are esteemed in the number of the impious and wicked: all shun them, and avoid their society and conversation, lest they receive some evil from their contact; nor is justice administered to them when seeking it, nor is any honour bestowed on them."

Given that Celticity came to Britain 'from the west' along the Atlantic seaboard lines of communication, and yet Druidry developed in Britain and was then pushed back 'into the west' along those same lines of Atlantic seaboard communication—and expanding into all of the Celtic climes of that age as they all pressed eastwards into central Europe—then we need to ask ourselves how important Druidry was to Celticity's actual survival.

Caesar also gives us a glimpse of this:

- "Over these Druids presides one who is invested with supreme authority among them. At his death, if any one of the rest is of superior dignity, he succeeds; but if there are many equal, the election is made by the suffrages of the Druids; sometimes they even contend for the presidency with arms."

Conflating all of these quotes together under the realisation that as "Judges of The Law" *et al*, the druids had even acquired that part of a king's sovereignty that yielded this right to the Arch-Druid—and thus, to the hierarchy of druids over which he presided—then it is quite clear that Britain's "Arthurianism" had subsumed Celticity, rather than the other way around.

Which is to say, Arthurianism was so strong that it became Celticity's administrating master!

The quintessential relationship between Merlin and Arthur exemplifies a modern-day expression that encapsulates the relationship between Druidry and Celticity.

This relationship illustrates a clear type of "church and state" separation but instead demarked as "**doctrine** and **warrior-defender of doctrine**":

- As the Arch Druid, Merlin represents the administrator of the repository of all doctrine, while Arthur, as king, is the Arch-Warrior who defends that doctrine and the realm it prevails over.

This symbiotic relationship shows that *preserving* knowledge and wisdom was vested in the Arch Druid while *protecting* these ideals was vested in the king and his warriors.

This is the point where we must ask ourselves what knowledge and wisdom a Celtic king was responsible for protecting, and here we have little choice but to revert to the etymology of the word druid, **which even before becoming Celtic** meant "Oak-Knower."

Naturally, we are rapidly converging on what the **awen** of being an Oak-Knower meant!

We've already summarised this as being 'the nation of oaken-family trees' that can be represented by the *awen* of being a Great Arthurian Forrest—and this comes down to the everyday reality of protecting every ninth-or-more generation native of a kingdom, as well as those who had been in a nation for more than three generations ~ including the right for all of these people to be allocated free land, based upon **birthright**.

So, how should we summarise 'the prevailing significance of the Oak-Knowers'?

Druidry itself was vested in the Ascent of Arthurian Britain, and just like the need to drink water is common to all mankind, the Celtic world realised that Britain's **Arthurian practice of Druidry** was quintessentially most important to successfully administer every precept of what it was to be Celtic—which in doing so, introduced and thus naturalised Britain's Arthurianism as being a Celtic trait that was administered by designated officers of Britain's introduced Druidic class.

Naturally, the whole question of 'chicken and egg' expands this conversation into the realm of wondering if Britain's primordial Arthurian development was merely a case of Celticity spontaneously spawning in Britain whilst 'Celticity from the west' simultaneously spread along the Atlantic Seaboard lines of communication towards it—which if being so would put the ilk of Cunliffe and Koch to consider even how much further back in time Celticity actually originated, versus when it is presently thought of having later been.

This could put the spawning of some Celtic traits in Britain farther back than 5,000 BC, and that's quite significant because the closer back towards 6,170 BC that Britain's Arthurian, even Celtic origin, is thought to be, then the closer we get to the living memory of the tsunami of the Storegga Slide having had such an impact on the British psyche that it became ingrained in the character of the natives of this land "to always get from one side of adversity" to the other, to always value the high ground.

That is, the further back Arthurian Celticity is determined to have existed in Britain, the closer we get to not just Britain's own "Great Flood" origin story, but also to the origin of the mandate of the "Crux of Arthurian Britain": the awen expressed in the prophecy that "Arthur will return as a raven."

169

Curiously, linguists often think that the historical defining nature of being a Celt was their capacity to speak a Celtic language.

Yet, to the contrary, the matter that Celticity adopted Arthurian Druidic practices not only expanded that lingual trait to include the expanded practices that Druidry imported **into** the Celtic world, it also raises the question of whether the primordial Arthurian origin of Druidry in Britain can be argued as being intrinsically Celtic itself, even before Proto-Celtic started to be spoken in Britain.

The Ascent of Arthurian Britain from the melt of the last ice age, 12,500 years ago, to the present, might even draw them towards the proposition that Celticity was spawned spontaneously in the northern and southern climes of The West—in Britain at the north of that west, and along the Iberian peninsular, at the south of that west.

This concept warrants a little expansion!

The origin of Druidry in Britain can be traced back to a primordial Arthurian source, which pre-dates the arrival of Proto-Celtic language and culture in Britain. It posits that the Arthurian Druidic practices were adopted and expanded by Celtic culture, raising the possibility that these practices were inherently part of the British tradition even before the Proto-Celtic influence.

In simpler terms, the "Primordial Arthurian origin of Druidry in Britain" refers to the idea that Druidic traditions and practices in Britain have deep, unique, and ancient roots tied to Arthurian legend or culture. These roots existed independently of the Celtic influence, implying that Druidry in Britain may have a distinct and ancient origin that is intrinsically British rather than solely a result of later Celtic integration. This is a testament to the rich and diverse heritage of Britain.

Although this topic needs further exploration to distinguish between certainty, probability, and mere possibility, one thing is quite certain:

- The Druidic nature of Arthurianism originated in Britain and spread from Britain into every existing Celtic clime, a fact that inspires awe and wonder at the far-reaching influence of this ancient tradition.

The significance of this is less the accolade to Britain and more the opportunities that prevail in every wider Celtic clime—it effectively means that every clime with Celtic heritage can claim a pre-supposed destiny that its indigenous natives—as part of The Great Arthurian Forrest—should ordinarily receive land for free by Celtic birthright.

This is quite significant, and in this modern day the leaders of the European Union have to concede that when the Common Market was first set up, its politicians frequently quoted that the widespread ancient distribution of Celts right across Europe indicated the high value it placed on the unity of Celtic ideals across Europe being a maxim that was to be respected—and yet, now, fifty years later, the EU has made no progress towards its 'citizens' acquiring free land by birthright, just as the ancient Arthurian practice extolled; to the contrary, the EU seems bent on resettling refugees from outside Europe at the expense of Europe's Celtic heritage.

You can't claim the benefits of Celticity without promoting the intrinsic nature of Celticity!

Despite this, it is clear that where the heritage of the last 12,500 years of Britain is 'the soil' from which 'The

Great Arthurian Forrest' sprang, there is nothing wrong with a Celt anywhere from claiming nourishment from this soil on the basis that 'The Roots' of all 'Oaken Trees' are intertwined with all of the other roots of all of the Oaken Trees of the whole Arthurian Forrest!

Conclusion

From the melt of the last ice age to the leading edge of "The Present"—where we continually take progressive step-by-step increments towards our predestined Arthurian Future—this is "The Soil" of all three—the history of our past, the 'projected history' of our present, and the 'predestined history' of our future—in which all Arthurian growth was predestined by the Four Great Prophecies of Arthurian Britain to spring forth!

Focus
In the midst of all this detail, let's not lose

sight of the fact that we need to cover all the background necessary to decypher Edward the Confessor's Deathbed Dream at the start of 1066 AD.

In this chapter, we have discussed The Secret Cypher of "The Soil" that The Great British Oak is rooted in.

In the next chapter, we will discuss The Secret Cypher of "The Roots" of The Great British Oak, discovering how they interweave with the roots of all other Oaken Trees in The Great Arthurian Forrest and where those roots came from!

In progressive chapters, we will then discuss the Secret Cyphers of "The Trunk", "The Branches", and "The Fruit".

That means we are just four chapters from discussing the dream itself—and none of these chapters will be as long as this chapter was!

For a fuller explanation about The Great Arthurian Forrest and its oaken nature—including a detailed account of the Awen of Camelot—please add *The Secret Cypher of Chalice Well* to your reading list.

Chapter Four

The Secret Cypher of The Roots

The Birth of an Oaken Tree With a Very Unique Destiny

Historical circumstances that can be represented by "The Roots" of 'The Great Old British Oak', how they took root in "The Soil", and indeed, where those roots came from.

We are on a quest to discover the finer details of the 'Great Old British Oak' that William the Conqueror cut down in 1066.

Curiously, this grand old tree had been the primary feature of the dream that Edward the Confessor had previously had when he was lying on his deathbed during the very same year that the Conqueror had invaded Britain.

As Secret Cypher Super Sleuths, we want to use the Science of Secret Cyphers to break The Secret Cypher of The Great Old British Oak into additional Cyphers.

The reason we want to do that is so that we can discover all of these Secret Cypher's finely interleaved details, and where in the previous chapter, we discussed **The Secret Cypher of "The Soil"** that this grand old oaken tree is rooted, in this chapter, we are going to resolve **The Secret Cypher of "The Roots"** of that grand old tree.

Where the Cypher of "The Soil" revealed the 12,500 years of British History that this 'oaken tree' was rooted, in this chapter, we are going to discuss "The Roots" of The Great Old British Oak, how they took root in "The Soil," and where those roots came from.

Inception

The Great Old British Oak is not just any tree. Because of its significance and stature since maturing, we should realise that despite it being just one tree in the midst of The Great Arthurian Forrest, many names could be applied to it.

These illustrate how well it stood out amongst the other trees that had also taken root in the same 12,500 years of the history of the 'Briton Soil' of mainland Great Britain—nobody could deny that by the time William the Conqueror cut down this Great Old British Oak in 1066, it had become so wonderful that it could only be expressed in superlatives that illustrate the stark contrast of how its silhouette loomed over the forrest.

Here, I'm going to wax lyrical, and

although some of these descriptions might seem a little hyperbolic, here at the outset, it shan't be very long before each and every one of them will be seen as perfectly expressed:
:

- A Verdant Monolith of Grandeur,
- The Epicentre of Arboreal Splendour,
- Nature's Crown Jewel,
- A Majestic Sentinel,
- A Living Tapestry of the Seasons,
- The Exalted Arboreal Luminary, and even
- A Celestial Pillar.

In short, The Great Old British Oak was already polling as "Number One" in The Great Arthurian Forrest of Britain—and in time, she would become the most significant oaken tree worldwide, even affecting how foreign governments structured themselves!

Predestined to be '**The Anointed One of The Forrest**', she had been planted in a strategic clearing in that forrest.

Her roots had grown deeply to become intertwined with the existing roots of the other Oaken Trees of The Great Arthurian Forrest, and when she came of age, she was anointed with the name of "Britannia".

Even the Romans foretold that she would take root in this fertile land, personifying her as a goddess armed with a spear and shield and wearing a Corinthian helmet.

Then, when the Romans declined in Britain and ultimately left, the Anglo-Saxons spied on this vacant, already furrowed Roman field, doing so from afar—who decided that it was there in that furrowed Roman field that they would plant their own roots.

In time, those Anglo-Saxon 'roots' would grow to become an 'Oaken Tree', and the edge of The Great Arthurian Forrest that surrounded that field would creep closer and closer to that Anointed Tree so that all of their roots would, in time, become interwoven.

In time, this 'Great Old Oaken Tree' would be cut down—as foretold in Edward the Confessor's Deathbed Dream—yet "at a distance of three furlongs", green branches would re-attach themselves to the roots of the tree and flourish by their own accord—which is to say, "the cut-down tree would be restored, "The Anointed One" would be brought back to life and bring prosperity to the land".

The Fertility of The Soil

Planting a tree with the goal of making it an arboreal trophy requires a prevailing hand capable of waltzing with destiny.

Although the Romans finally left Britain around 410 AD, the decline of the

Roman Empire had started much earlier.

Magnus Maximus, who died in 388 AD, was the last Roman emperor to exercise direct imperial control over Roman Britain. It is thought that he appointed Coel Hen as the last *Dux Britanniarum*—Duke of Britain—perhaps sometime around 380 AD.

Coel Hen is the "Old King Cole" of our nursery rhymes, and the reason why "Old King Cole was a merry old soul" was that as the Roman Empire declined in Britain, Coel Hen was able to have a prevailing hand over the restoration of native Britain.

Of course, Coel Hen did not prevail as Duke of Britain over the whole of Britain; he only prevailed over the centre.

Yet, as every military commander knew, to control the centre of Britain was to control Britain itself, and as the Roman Empire declined in the centre, the native kingdoms in the centre rose. Coel Hen's territories even included the henge called King Arthur's Round Table!

Curiously, it was the tribe that the Romans called the Carvetii which was the guardian of the henge—who, as heirs of "The Risen Stags" of Star Carr, were known as 'The Stag People'—who once again rose to become the most powerful kingdom in Britain under the lineage of Coel Hen's descendants.

This kingdom became known as the Kingdom of *Rheged*—the "Kingdom of Gifts" or the "Kingdom of Gifted Prosperity".

The Age of Arthur is considered to have started in 350 AD, with the decline of the Roman Empire translating to the ascent of a revived native Britain.

It was the Kingdom of Rheged that had once again become "The Risen Stags" of Britain!

Yet the Kingdom of Rheged was just one kingdom that Coel Hen's heirs administered, and you'll remember that this region's name is traditionally translated from Welsh as "The Old North"—it occupies an approximate area of 125 miles from the henge, King Arthur's Round Table.

Although this radius of 125 miles from the henge is a good approximation, it should be remembered that this figure is only a rule of thumb.

In some places, that radius extended further—such as incorporating all of the Kingdom of Gwynedd in the now north of Wales—and indeed, including all of the north of Wales itself!

Yet in other places, it extended not nearly as far as 125 miles from the henge, perhaps marginally less.

For example, it included the lands of the Manaw Gododdin on Edinburgh's side of the Firth of Forth but probably did not extend northward over the firth to the Manaw's Roman-era territories, which, although thought to extend to Clackmannan, are not thought to have extended as far north as over the river Tay to Dundee, which is precisely 125 miles from King Arthur's Round Table.

Indeed, historians need a deft hand when trying to determine exactly where the border of Yr Hen Ogledd finished In some places.

For example, the northern end of that Roman road called Dere Street does cross the river Tay near Dundee—suggesting a relationship with the Manaw Gododdin north of the firth, however, the road was fortified that far north, suggesting that it was penetrating the region of the Picts by then, who were to the north of the Manaw Gododdin.

The Romans had been friendly with the Gododdin—known to them as the Votadini—but were not friendly with the Picts!

Similarly, in the south of Yr Hen Ogledd, the Kingdom of Elmet is thought to have its southern border around the river Sheaf, and although this places the city of Sheffield inside Yr Hen Ogledd, the most southern reach of the Sheaf is only 104 miles from the henge.

By similar tokens, the city of Hull is inside Yr Hen Ogledd, however the Kingdom of Lindsey, which was just south of Hull, across the river Humber, was not originally in Yr Hen Ogledd— and that part of the southern shore of the Humber that formed the border with Lindsey to its south is only around 115 miles from the henge.

Although Lindsey was absorbed into Deira by the 7th century, it alternated between being subjugated by Deira and Mercia, so whilst under Deira it was in Yr Hen Ogledd's orbit, but whilst under Mercia, it was not.

This does, however, put the full east coast, from the river Humber up to the southern shore of the Firth of Forth—including Edinburgh—inside Yr Hen Ogledd.

When looking at maps of that general period it is important to realise that before the Anglo-Saxons arrived, the whole of Yr Hen Ogledd was under Coel Hen and his indigenous Briton descendants.

This includes Glasgow in the north-west of Yr Hen Ogledd, and the whole of the west coast of mainland Scotland down to where it meets the Cumberland coast.

On page 50, there's a diagram of the time-line of The Age of Arthur, charts of Coel Hen's lineage on Pages 52 and 53, and a map of Coel Hen's expanded territories on Page 54, which illustrates the region of Yr Hen Ogledd.

The cautious view is that after the Romans left Britain around 410 AD, "The Soil" was completely fertile for the indigenous "Great Arthurian Forrest" to prosper.

In this context, this "soil" was filled with 'The Roots' of the myriad of 'Oaken Family Trees' of every indigenous Briton nation that was under the authority of Coel Hen and his descendants—and because all of these 'Oaken Trees' made up the 'Great Arthurian Forrest', their 'roots' were fully intertwined with each other!

On a side-note, I am hoping that you are visualising "The Great Arthurian Forrest" from the personal perspective where each 'oaken family tree' is headed by a pencenedl who is the patriarch of a family that has a pedigree that is at least nine generations deep, and that each family tree's collateral branches are at most nine branches wide—this is the very reason that this awen was expressed in the first place—don't forget that the druids had been known as "Oak-Knowers" since much earlier ancient times!

With this in mind, we can remember that the Anglo-Saxons didn't arrive in Britain "to lay their roots down" until around 449 AD—so if "The Soil" was completely fertile for the 'Great Arthurian Forrest' to prosper from 410 AD, then what happened that allowed the Anglo-Saxons in?

The Prophecy of Bran

Bran the Blessed was Britain's original warrior-patron saint. His name, Bran, means "raven"—which illustrates that even the Celts of Britain had adopted the symbol of the raven by the time of his ministry in the first century!

It was from Bran the Blessed that we get the first of the Four Great Prophecies of Arthurian Britain, which is known as the Prophecy of Bran:

- So long as the head of Bran faces south on Britain's white mount, Britain will be protected.

The Welsh manuscript, the Mabinogion, lists the first-century king of the Catuvellauni tribe, the famous King Caratacus, as the son of Bran the Blessed.

Curiously, in later centuries, this first of the Four Great Prophecies of Arthurian Britain—this "Prophecy of Bran"—would evolve into the fourth of these great prophecies:

- So long as there are ravens in the Tower of London, England would be protected.

In this book, I'm more interested in extolling how the Prophecy of Bran illustrates why the Anglo-Saxons managed to gain such a significant foothold in Britain that they were able to "lay down their own roots" in "the soil of Britain".

However, if you want further information about why there are ravens in The Tower of London, I'd recommend that you start off by reading my first book in this series, "The Secret Cypher of Chalice Well", and you then progress to reading my third book in this series, which I plan to be "The Secret Cypher of Why There Are Ravens in The Tower of London".

As you can appreciate, I've already cracked that Secret Cypher and that third book of this series should follow hot on the heels of this one!

Although I'll just touch the surface here, even The Prophecy of Bran is a Secret Cypher, so I'll treat it as one.

The back-story to the prophecy is

that when Bran lay dying and his death was imminent, he instructed his fellow warriors that when he died, they should place his head on "Britain's White Mount facing south", who in saying so uttered the prophecy "So long as my head faces south on Britain's White Mount, Britain will be protected!"

From this, we get the prophecy: "So long as the Head of Bran faces South on Britain's White Mount, Britain will be protected!"

This prophecy is merely Bran's original first-person expression transposed to be expressed as third-person.

Introducing The Secret Cypher of The Prophecy of Bran

This Secret Cypher draws on three other Secret Cyphers that were implied by its wording:

1. The Secret Cypher of "The Raven"—determined by Bran's name meaning 'raven';
2. The Secret Cypher of "The South"; and,
3. The Secret Cypher of "The White Mount".

Although I discussed the first two of these at length in my book *The Secret Cypher of Chalice Well*, we have sufficiently touched on these in this book to enable us to rewrite the prophecy as follows:

- So long as The Head of the Raven faces South on Britain's White Mount, Britain will be protected.

Here, we need to treat this prophecy with reverence for the matter that Bran was a Christian saint, so as such, the prophecy's interpretation must not only be consistent with Christian ideals but also—because Bran was, in effect, "The Patron Saint of Britain"— then his expression of this prophecy must be regarded as being evangelical.

Yet, on what basis can we call Bran the Patron Saint of Britain?

The answer to this is quite easy, and that's because the part of the prophecy that said, "So long as…" proves that Bran had entered into a covenant with God on behalf of the Britons:

- So long as [the terms of the covenant], Britain will be protected.

So, in the same sense of the Jewish parallel where it can be said:

- "Moses entered into a covenant with God on behalf of the Israelites, establishing a sacred agreement that governed their relationship and obligations to each other".

then it can equally be said that:

- "Bran the Blessed entered into a covenant with God on behalf of the Britons, establishing a sacred agreement that governed their relationship and obligations to each other".

As such, the aim of solving "The Secret Cypher of The Prophecy of Bran" is to resolve what that covenant is.

Although I am 'High Church of England' in matters of faith, I did have the pleasure of attending a Pentecostal Bible College in Australia during my late twenties—Harvest Bible College, in the State of Victoria. I was registered there under my Russian and Polish titles, Count Ossalinsky and Count Ossolinski, respectively.

All of these many years later, I still remember the subject of "Hermeneutics" quite well, and it can be described as follows:

- Hermeneutics is the theory and

methodology of interpretation, especially the interpretation of written texts, like religious scriptures, literary works, legal documents, and philosophical writings. It's concerned with how we understand and interpret the meaning of texts, particularly those that are open to various interpretations or have deeper layers of meaning.

Although I am applying the Science of Hermeneutics to actual biblical concepts—my liberty to do so is because Bran the Blessed was a Christian warrior-saint—the science is not specifically tied to religious studies and can apply to any branch of philosophy.

• Hermeneutics can, indeed, be applied to interpreting any written text!

As such, the Science of Hermeneutics is part of your "Science of Secret Cyphers Tool-kit", which gives you another keyword to research to increase your skill at interpreting Secret Cyphers!

Firstly—as previously discussed—the symbol of the raven distils to imply that the role of the raven is "to get from one side of adversity to the other".

We drew this conclusion from the raven's appearance in the story about The Great Flood in the Book of Genesis!

The significant thing about the covenant is that it uses the condition "So long as..." in a statement that is applied to a raven—on the one hand, the raven will always get from one side of adversity to the other—yet on the other hand, the condition "So long as ..." restricts the capability of the raven from getting to the other side of that adversity!

How do we resolve this conflict?

More broadly, how do we rationalise the promise that, as ravens, we will get from one side of adversity to the other, with the rationale that under the circumstance that "The Head of The Raven does not face south," we might not be protected?

1. If the promise is that 'as ravens' we will always get from one side of adversity to the other side of it, then it can only be that under the terms of the covenant, that if we are not faithful to facing south for a time then God will allow us to be unprotected to discipline us.
2. Yet when we address this so that "The Head of the Raven" once again continues to face south, then in time, we will get to the other side of the adversity—where God will again protect us!

At this stage, these suppositions are merely academic, so let's look further and try and resolve what The Secret Cypher of "The Head of The Raven" means—but doing it in the context of what The Secret Cypher of "The South" means!

The Secret Cypher of The South

This Secret Cypher has a very wide breadth, so in this book, I'm going to cherry-pick a few key components from my explanation about it in my book, "The Secret Cypher of Chalice Well".

In that book, I explained how our ancient ancestors believed that their inspiration came from *The Source* of The Unseen South.

Whether I would draw on Welsh awen to explain this—or even use a modern-day allegory—the simple matter was that when our ancient ancestors faced the rising sun in the east, then the north was to their left, and the south was to their right.

"The Birth of British Symbolism" dia-

gram on Page 81 expresses this concept.

This relates to The Prophecy of Bran
because, in our ancestors' Brittonic
tongue, the words for North and Left
were the same, as were the words for
South and Right.

- **Gogledd**: North, Left; mutates as
  Ogledd.
- **De:** South, Right, mutates as Dde.

This means that whenever we consider ancient Welsh manuscripts,
prophecies, and even Expressions
of Awen, we should always consider substituting the word North with
Left (and vice versa) and South with
Right (and vice versa) to see if doing
so gives us better meaning.

Let's consider what facing "The
South" might mean in the Prophecy
of Bran, as well as facing "The Right".

In short, we are now applying the

Science of Hermeneutics to two expressions:

1. So long as The Head of The Raven Faces **"The South"**, Britain will be protected.
2. So long as The Head of The Raven Faces **"The Right"**, Britain will be protected.

On the one hand, some might think that the expression, "So long as The Head of The Raven Faces 'The South', ..." could translate as, "So long as The Head of The Raven Faces 'France', ..."—however, this is a false trap that many historians have fallen into—even some of the earliest written Welsh prose is liable to be misinterpreted, having transposed various ancient prophecies into stories that make them easier to be handed down.

For example, in the Second Book of The Mabinogion:

- Ac yna y peris Bendigeidfran lladd ei benn. 'A chymerwch chwi y pen,' heb ef, 'a dygwch hyd y Gwyn-fryn yn Llundain, a chleddwch â'i wyneb ar Ffrainc ef.

and this translates as:

- And then Bran ordered his head to be cut off. 'And take the head,' he said, 'and carry it to the white hill in London, and bury it with its face towards France.'

As 12th-century prose, this was an entirely true statement, yet it becomes a 'castle of clouds' when used as a replacement for the original prophecy.

Here, the danger is that one could quite easily digress from the intent of the original prophecy to imply that France was Britain's natural enemy, merely because Bran's head was facing that way.

For a start, France did not exist in the first century, yet significantly, why would God enter into a covenant that only protected us from one direction?

What about The Head of The Raven facing the northeast to protect us from the Vikings, or facing the west to protect us from the Scoti?

The thing that many historians have overlooked is wondering what this prophecy would have meant to the Christian Patron saint who expressed it!

1. What does facing "**The** South" mean to a Christian?
2. What does facing "**The** Right" mean to a Christian?

The two obvious answers to these questions are sublime, and as it turns out, considering both options yields the same answer!

Where should a Christian get his inspiration?

Isn't *The Source* of The Unseen South known to Christians as The Holy Spirit?

• That goes a long way toward explaining the prophecy that prevails in many modern-day Christian circles: "Seek the Great Southland of The Holy Spirit!"

Similarly—by considering that "The Right" can be an alternative to "The South" when translating old manuscripts from Welsh—let's consider who sits at *The Right* hand of The Father, who after the Last Supper said that he had to rise into heaven so that The Holy Spirit could come.

That was Christ, of course—but in having said so, it is clear that to a first-century Briton saint, that expressions of faithfully facing "The Right", and faithfully facing "The

South" would both be directly associated with 'facing' The Holy Spirit.

Keep in mind that the reason why I am going into such religious depth as this is because we are trying to determine how a first-century Christian saint would have interpreted this prophecy—we are not doing a bible-study per se.

So, this is where the solution to the Secret Cypher of "The Head of The Raven" becomes obvious, with the prophecy being translated by the following four steps:

1. So long as the head of Bran faces south on Britain's White Mount, Britain will be protected!
2. So long as The Head of The Raven faces South (or Right) on Britain's White Mount, Britain will be protected!
3. So long as The Leadership of Britain ("The Head of The Raven") faces South (or Right) on Britain's

White Mount, Britain will be protected!

4. So long as The Leadership of Britain faces The Holy Spirit on Britain's White Mount, Britain will be
protected!

This leaves us with the simple matter of resolving "The Secret Cypher
of The White Mount".

The awen of this is easy to determine,
and that's because it is expressed as
"Britain's" White Mount. This expression obviously alludes to the practice
of 'ascending the white hill', which
relates to the ascent of holiness!

Curiously, this qualifies the covenant further because it means that
it is not enough for "The Leadership
of Britain to face The Holy Spirit "—it
means that in doing so, the Leadership of Britain" must also be dedicat-
ed to ascending 'the hill of holiness'.

Although many readers will be satisfied with this explanation of the prophecy, it has a sublime, scintillating aspect!

When Bran's head was placed on "Britain's White Mount" facing south, soon after his death in the first century, his faithful companion warriors placed it on "The White Hill" in London.

If you didn't know, that's the name of the hill that the Tower of London is on, and indeed, the name of The Tower of London is "The White Tower", which is named after the hill that it stands on.

If you are interested in discovering how "The Prophecy of Bran" evolved into "So long as there are Ravens in the Tower of London, England will be protected!", then look out for my next book, which I plan to be "The Secret Cypher of Why There Are Ravens in The Tower of London".

How Did the Anglo-Saxons Put Down Their Roots in Britain

Having discussed The Prophecy of Bran, it is quite clear that from around 449 AD, when the Anglo-Saxons started their invasions of Britain, that Britain was not being protected by the Covenant of Bran.

Because God is faultless, we can only conclude that the leadership of our ancient Briton ancestors had not been faithful to "facing The South (or The Right)".

Their unfaithfulness in this matter must have been so broad that God must have decided to 'discipline his Briton children' by allowing the Anglo-Saxons to teach them a lesson.

Of course, we must regard this in the limited sense of this act being disciplinary, and because God's covenant was with 'ravens', it meant that we would, in time, get to the other side of all adversity—which means that in time, we would break free from the Anglo-Saxon yoke.

Naturally, this 'breaking free' is a story for another time, but it should not be overlooked that even the Prophecy of Bran is in accord with the core substance of The Four Great Prophecies of Arthurian Britain.

Indeed, the wording of Edward the Confessor's Deathbed Dream even illustrates that God knew of the Anglo-Saxons' great sins, and the dream's fulfilment can be read as entirely consistent with the Four Great Prophecies of Arthurian Britain!

Although God's practice of taking us to task over not being faithful to the Covenant of Bran is really just God trying to teach us to remedy this situation, let's not forget that the Anglo-Saxon invasions were not the first reminder that God had been spoon-feeding us since Bran arranged that covenant with God.

- Not too long after Bran died, the Romans invaded, illustrating that The Leadership of Britain had not yet become fully faithful to him.

How many times do we have to learn the lesson that not only does the leadership of Britain have to 'face south' so that Britain is protected, but it must also 'ascend the white hill of holiness' in the process?

The Roots of The Great Old British Oak

Quite clearly, The Great Arthurian Forrest was well established by the time that the Anglo-Saxons laid down their oaken roots in Britain.

Yet the Anglo-Saxon's roots did indeed take hold, and over time it was these roots that grew into The Great Old British Oak that William the Conqueror cut down in 1066.

Despite having Anglo-Saxon roots, how did this 'great oaken tree' grow to acquire such significant stature so that in a future age, it would not only conform to the fulfilment of The Four Great Prophecies of Arthurian Britain, but as "Britannia" it would be seen as an indigenous oak that would be the pride of The Great Arthurian Forrest itself?

To answer this question, we need to continue on our merry journey by discussing "The Trunk" that raised The Tree's branches so high that the tree itself was tallest in the forrest.

We are now only three chapters away from discussing Edward the Confessor's Deathbed Dream itself, but first, we need to discuss:

1. The Secret Cypher of "The Trunk" of The Great Old British Oak;
2. The Secret Cypher of "The Branches" of The Great Old British Oak; and,

3. The Secret Cypher of "The Fruit" of The Great Old British Oak—its crop of acorns.

Tally-ho, good and faithful steed!

Chapter Five

The Secret Cypher of The Trunk

The Character of an Oaken Tree With a Very Special Destiny

Historical circumstances that can be represented by "The Trunk" of 'The Great Old British Oak', leading to how its branches were able to take their characters from "The Trunk" of this very special oaken tree.

We have previously discussed 12,500 years of British history, which, using a Welsh Expression of Awen, we described as "The Soil", in which The Great Old British Oak is rooted.

From there, we discussed the circumstances in which the Anglo-Saxons were able to lay down their own 'roots' in Britain, using a similar Expression of Awen that described those Anglo-Saxon roots reaching deeply into British soil as being "'The Roots' of The Great Old British Oak"— whose roots began to become thoroughly intertwined with the roots of "The Great Arthurian Forrest"!

We are, of course, on a quest to discover the finer details of the 'Great Old British Oak' that William the Conqueror cut down in 1066. This chapter will explore the awen of "The Trunk" of that Great Old British Oak.

As such, we'll discuss how 'The Roots' in this very special "Soil" gave 'The Trunk' its own very special character!

That, in turn, will lay the basis of the next chapter, where we will discuss how "The Trunk" supported "The Branches" of this age-old, anointed oaken tree, including how those branches were characterised by the nutrients that the roots drew from the soil.

Naturally, 'The Branches of The Tree' are supported by 'The Trunk of the Tree'.

So, as we progress to later chapters, we'll start discovering "why God's prevailing hand" caused William the Conqueror to cut down the tree in the first place—and how its restoration "three furlongs distant", as prophesied by Edward the Confessor's Deathbed Dream, fits in with the fulfilment of The Four Great Prophecies of Arthurian Britain.

Where The Roots Meet the Trunk

Although The Roots of The Great Old British Oak came from broad Anglo-Saxon climes, by the time they drew so close to each other as to formulate themselves into The Trunk that became The Tree, it is very curious that The Roots themselves can be characterised as only being Saxon.

This is exemplified by Athelstan, King of Wessex—who, being from Wessex, was 'King of the West Saxons—who, in 926 AD, formed The Kingdom of England at the henge King Arthur's Round Table.

Here, the Saxons can be seen as having triumphed over every other invading kingdom that had laid down roots in Great Britain since the Romans left in 410 AD, and that's because none of the Anglo-Saxon kingdoms that were under his authority ever broke away from being under the dominance of his crown.

Although we usually say that the "Anglo-Saxons" began invading Great Britain from around 449 AD, the simple matter is that a broader description of those invaders includes those who—in a clockwise direction around the coast of the North Sea—

were the Jutes, Angles, Saxons, Frisii, and Franks.

The various kingdoms these invaders created in Great Britain were, over time, all formulated into what became known as the Anglo-Saxon *Heptarchy*.

Although the term Heptarchy implies the existence of seven kingdoms, it has effectively become a term of convenience because the actual number of kingdoms under the Anglo-Saxon High Kings fluctuated over time.

Nevertheless, one might regard the distant tips of The Roots of The Great Old British Oak as having been Jute, Angle, Saxon, Frisian, and Frank.

By the time of 'The Heptarchy', the challenge of which nationality would eventually prevail over them all can be seen in the rise of the Office of the Anglo-Saxon "High King"—the Bretwalda.

217

The Old English term Bretwalda—usually translated into English as High King—was still used by Athelstan, the first King of the English, in the tenth century.

From time to time, High Kings changed as one or another kingdom broke away from being under the existing High King.

When a kingdom broke away from being under the High King, the Office of "High King" was relegated into 'abatement' until once again all of the Heptarchy was under another single High King—who, prevailing over all of the Heptarchy, brought the Office of High King back out of abatement.

Here, the word *abatement* merely means the temporary suspension or reduction in the powers, duties, or effectiveness of the Office of High King.

The most famous Anglo-Saxon High King was Oswiu, whose brother Oswald was the 6th Anglo-Saxon High King.

Although Oswiu eventually became the 7th Anglo-Saxon High King after his brother, Oswald, the 6th High King, died, the transition from Oswald as the 6th to Oswiu as the 7th was not automatic.

On the one hand, Oswald had been killed by the sub-king, Penda, King of the Mercians—who, in killing the High King, broke away from the Office of High King, drawing that Office into abatement.

Yet, on the other hand, it took Oswiu thirteen years to bring all of the Heptarchy back under his dominion, elevating his family line back into the rarefied air of that high Office.

These two Anglo-Saxon High Kings had become so on the ascent of the

Angle kingdoms of Bernicia and Deira, both of which were located on the eastern seaboard of Yr Hen Ogledd, The Old North. Both of these kingdoms are depicted in the map of Yr Hen Ogledd on Page 54.

Bernicia and Deira had been orbiting each other in a slow dance that eventually unified them to become the Kingdom of Northumbria!

The records of the Kings of Northumbria show its kings alternating between the Bernician and Deiran dynasties, which in time are merely shown as Northumbrian.

However, when the Danes invaded England, Bernicia in the north seemed to have acquired its independence again, if even as only a client kingdom of the Danes.

The Danes, of course, were heirs of the original Jutes of Jutland who had formed part of the Heptarchy, so when considering their impact upon the circumstances of The Great Old British Oak, they are easily considered as if part of the 'Anglo-Saxon' umbrella—the only difference between any of the original Jutes, Angles, Saxons, Frisii, and Franks, was that the Danes, as the next-generation *rulers of Jutland*, were merely another wave of assailants but who were nevertheless the same folk as the first generation of assailants upon Britain, coming from that very same region's heirs.

Yet it was Oswiu's marriage to Rhiainfellt, the heiress Queen of Rheged, in 638 that exemplifies how powerful it was to prevail over the centre of mainland Great Britain.

This is because by the time Oswiu became the 7th Anglo-Saxon High King, he not only controlled Rheged, which was the Guardian of the Henge at Great Britain's very centre, who by prevailing over the majority of Yr

Hen Ogledd at the start of his quest to become High King, had effectively anointed Yr Hen Ogledd as his platform to bring all of the Heptarchy in submission to him.

Oswiu, his brother, Oswald, and Edwin, the previous King of Northumbria, are all saints of the church.

The birthplace of the Church of England wasn't in the south of England, it was created in Yr Hen Ogledd in the year 664 when Oswiu convened the Synod of Whitby!

Yet from the time Athelstan, the King of Wessex, created the Kingdom of England at the henge in 926 AD, none of the kingdoms of the Heptarchy ever again broke away from the crown of the King of England.

The House of Wessex continued holding the office of King of England down to 1013, when the House of Denmark took the throne for the period of 1013 to 1014, however the House of Wessex wrenched it back in 1014 for two years, from which time the House of Denmark won it back for the period of 1016 until 1042, when Edward the Confessor became King of England.

Curiously, these struggles between the Houses of Wessex and Denmark were not like previous cases where individual Anglo-Saxon kingdoms had fought to break away from the Office of Anglo-Saxon High King—the Wessex/Denmark endeavours were not campaigns to break away from the Office of the High King, but instead, to take the High King's crown for themselves!

As such, the Office of High King did not go into abatement when one of the Houses of Wessex or Denmark subjugated the other; instead, the Crown of England itself was yielded to the prevailing house at any particular point in time of these struggles.

During this phase of the development of The Great Old British Oak, the struggle was really about which of the Anglo-Saxon roots would be the prevailing root to which all of the other roots would attach themselves.

It would be this prevailing Root that would singularly be attached to The Trunk of The Tree, which in turn would raise The Tree's branches high over the rest of The Great Arthurian Forrest!

As it turned out, it was "The Saxon Root" of the Kings of Wessex that prevailed over all of the other roots, and in that sense, despite The Root System of The Great Old British Oak having root tips that were originally Jute, Angle, Saxon, Frisian, and Frank, by the time that the roots joined the trunk of that grand old tree, they were Saxon—and only Saxon!

Over a thousand years later—here, in the present day and with me being the master of this quill—the fact that only **Saxon Roots** joined to 'The Trunk' of The Great Old British Oak would have something to do with the fulfilment of Edward the Confessor's Deathbed Dream!

The Nature of "The Trunk"

Although we tend to describe The Great Old British Oak as an Oaken Tree, on what basis does The Tree's Root System prove that it is an oak species?

Of course, I could wax lyrical about the various cultures of the Saxons and those other peoples whose roots came from around the eastern and south-eastern rim of the North Sea; however, the proof is much closer to home.

When Athelstan formed the Kingdom of England at the henge in 926 AD, he did, of course, inherit the legacies of the previous Anglo-Saxon High

Kings—and the jewel of all of those was the Kingdom of Rheged, which the Office of High King had inherited from King Oswald when Rheged was articulated to Bernicia, just 288 years before in 638 AD.

The dynastic marriage of Rhiainfellt, the heiress Queen of Rheged, to Oswiu of Bernicia in 638 **articulated** the Kingdom of Rheged to the Office of the Anglo-Saxon High King.

Although at the time of the dynastic marriage, Oswiu was merely a prince of Bernicia, this meant that from the time of the marriage, he was the King of Rheged but based on Rhiainfellt's native right as its heiress queen.

Regrettably, our dear Rhiainfellt died only a few years later, and although she had first bore Oswiu a son who later ruled Bernicia (as well as a daughter), it was Oswiu who ruled Rheged in his own right from the time of Rhiainfellt's death.

Of course, when Oswiu's brother, Oswald, died just four years after that dynastic marriage, Oswiu was catapulted into being responsible for Bernicia, Deira, and Rheged.

Yet, by the time Oswiu was the 7th Anglo-Saxon High King, thirteen years later, he had the whole Heptarchy to rule over!

So, regarding the question of knowing that The Great Old British Tree is an oak, how does all of this fit in?

The answer lies in the relationship between the Kingdom of Rheged and the Crown of the Anglo-Saxon High King!

And—as always—this answer has to be in accord with the Four Great Prophecies of Arthurian Britain.

Firstly, we know that this great tree is rooted in "The Soil" of 12,500 years of The History of The Ascent of Arthurian Britain.

We also know that The Great Arthurian Forrest is also rooted in this "soil", and because "oaken family pedigrees" of nine generations are described by Welsh awen as being oaks—as exemplified by druids being "oak-knowers"—then we also know that all of the trees of The Great Arthurian Forrest are oaks.

Of course, we know that Arthur will return as a raven—which means that in time, indigenous Britain will be restored—yet we also know from Edward the Confessor's Deathbed Dream that The Great Old British Tree will also be restored to flourish by its own accord!

Because of that, we know that this Great Old British Oak has a place in The Great Arthurian Forrest!

Although the matter of being part of The Great Arthurian Forrest alludes to the tree being an oak, the inescapable truth is that because the Kingdom of Rheged was articulated to the Office of the Anglo-Saxon High King, then the allegiance of the Ravens of Rheged was *as if chained* to the Office of the Anglo-Saxon High King.

Because of that, one of the many "roots" that forms the basis of the root system of The Great Old British Tree is the matter of Rheged having been in servitude to the Anglo-Saxons—and this makes "The Rheged Root" one of those roots of the Great Old British Tree!

As the Kingdom of Rheged is part of The Great Arthurian Forrest, then by the definition of Rheged being indigenous, its root can only be that of an indigenous oak.

In conclusion, one can only suppose that if one root of a tree's root system is the root of an oak, then the rest of that tree's root system must also be the roots of an oak—which means that the tree itself can only be an oak.

The Sovereignty of "The Trunk"

It is fascinating to reflect on the issue of a Celtic nation's destiny having traditionally been based upon every ninth generation family head—whose 'family tree' consisted of 'branches' that were at most nine generations wide and nine generations deep—being qualified by that 'family tree' pedigree to sit in that Celtic Kingdom's national council.

Curiously, the fact that all of these "Oaken Family Trees" of The Great Arthurian Forrest have the right to sit as delegates in that nation's Celtic House of Lords tends to illustrate that these "Oaken Family Trees" are **not** the only "Oaken Trees" in The Great Arthurian Forrest!

On the one hand, we should have rev-

erence for these Oaken Trees repre-senting pedigrees!

The sublime thing about this is that:

1. The birthright of every Pencenedl to sit in a Celtic kingdom's House of Lords points directly to the existence of the pedigree of the king of that Celtic nation, which that Celtic kingdom's "House of Lords" serves!
2. How do we represent the pedigree of anyone in a Celtic kingdom who has a pedigree of nine generations or more—even the pedigree of the king? *As an Oaken Tree of The Great Arthurian Forrest!*

As such, *All of Awen* reveals to us that a Celtic nation can be visualised as all of the Oaken Family Trees of all of the Pencenedls who sit in that nation's House of Lords, surrounding an Oaken Tree of greater stature that represents the Oaken Pedigree of the king of that Kingdom!

Imagine an Oaken Forrest with a single Oaken Tree of greater stature at its centre, representing The King of that Forrest!

So, imagine that there were many Celtic kingdoms right across Britain.

How would you visualise that?

- In the Awen of a Forrest-of-Forrests, where as far as the eye could see, there were all The Oaken Family Trees of every ninth-generation family head who exists right across the land, there would also be various Oaken Family Trees of *Kings of those Forrests* interspersed right across the breadth of this "Great Arthurian Forrest-of-Forrests".

Yet we need to include an additional "Oaken Family Tree" at the centre of this 'forrest-of-forrests'—one with greater stature than even the oaken family trees of the kings of each Kingdom!

There, right in the middle of this for-rest of forrests, is The Great Old Brit-ish Oak!

The **Great Old British Oak** is **The Sov-ereign Tree** of **The Great Arthurian Forrest of Britain**, whose stature pre-vails over all of the other oaken trees of this forrest-of-forrests!

Naturally, I've appended "of Britain" to accommodate any Celtic Reviv-al that might occur in any country worldwide!

This **Sovereign Tree** of **The Great Ar-thurian Forrest of Britain** was once cut down by William the Conqueror in 1066—yet Edward the Confessor's previous Deathbed Dream prophe-sied that at 'three furlongs distance', green branches would reattach themselves to its root and flourish by their own accord!

What is the future of this *Verdant Monolith of Grandeur,* this *Epicen-*

233

tre of Arboreal Splendour, this *Crown Jewel of Nature*, this *Majestic Sentinel*, this *Living Tapestry of the Seasons*, this *Exalted Arboreal Luminary,* this *Celestial Pillar?*

- What are the implications of Edward the Confessor's Deathbed Dream being fulfilled?
- How does The Great Old British Oak fit in with The Four Great Prophecies of Arthurian Britain?

Having considered this "sovereign trunk", we will consider the tree's "sovereign branches" in the next chapter!

Tally-ho, good and faithful steed!

Chapter Six

The Secret Cypher of The Branches

'Characters' of an Oaken Tree With a Very Special Destiny!

"The Branches" of 'The Great Old British Oak' can be represented as actual historical pedigrees of various kings of England who have reigned since the tree first took root. Although these "Branches" take their character from "The Trunk" of this very special Oaken Tree, it is the series of sovereign kings and their particular Family-Tree Branches that are extolled by the canopy of this especially anointed tree—illustrating that these Family Tree branches always had a very special predestined purpose!

Why are we speaking about The History of Britain in terms of **Oaken Trees**

Flesch—57; Reading time—25:33; Speaking time—49:46

235

of The Great Arthurian Forrest?

Why do we extol this imagery as though it came out of the mysterious 'Cauldron of Awen' as a vision?

Why do we vest this doctrine with the historical Celtic Druid class being the 'Oak-Knowers' of our people"?

Although it is from the pedigrees of those with ninth-descent that Celtic Family Trees are each symbolised as an Oaken Tree of The Great Arthurian Forrest, the broader answer to these questions is twofold.

Firstly, when endeavouring to interpret Edward the Confessor's Deathbed Dream of the year 1066, we need to view the elements of that dream in the context of how those symbols were viewed **when** Edward the Confessor had that dream.

We should always remember that Edward is considered to be a saint in both the Roman Catholic Church and the Church of England, and because of this, his deathbed dream's interpretation needs to have reverence for the evangelical views of the church at large—but as they were during that same age.

Secondly—and perhaps most significantly—this symbolism aligns itself perfectly with the Christian evangelical symbols of awen that the indigenous natives of Britain had already built into their language as Secret Cyphers; their role was to carry the truth of these matters from generation to generation, from age to age, from millennia to millennia.

With all of this symbolism flying in ever-diminishing circles as though being cherished leaves caught up in the vortex of an autumn wind, let's not lose sight of the matter that Expressions of Awen **echo** the indigenous prophets of our past—such as Bran the Blessed in the 1st Century, and Aneirin and Taliesin in the 6th Century—therefore, no matter how these symbols are 'harvested as Oaken Leaves', we must interpret them in a manner that is consistent with The Four Great Prophecies of Arthurian Britain!

As such, it should be natural for us to continue to make Expressions of Awen using our everyday spoken word, and during such conversation, the symbols themselves should continue to be understood in the context in which they were originally expressed.

Continuing with these expressions in the context of illustrating the nature of The Great Old British Oak, it should not be overlooked that a very curious facet about an Oaken Tree is that The Trunk feeds The Branches with their essential nutrients, not The Roots!

Although The Roots endow The Tree

with its sovereign right to be a tree—exemplified by the genus of the Rheged Root defining this species of tree as an Oak—then despite that this tree's roots are intertwined with the Oaken Roots of the whole Arthurian Forrest, it is not 'The Root System' that 'The Branches' draw on to define their own peculiar significance, but instead 'The Trunk'.

Put into an 'Oaken perspective', it is 'The Trunk' that The Branches draw their nourishment from, which, in doing so, delivers The Nourishment that The Branches receive from The Roots into **The Trunk's** preordained context:

- In this context, it is The Trunk of The Tree that *raises the profile* of The Branches of this tree to be high above The Branches of the rest of the Great Arthurian Forrest of Britain—without The Trunk having raised The Branches to such an esteemed height, this tree would not be able to be distinguished from any regular tree in this vast Oaken Forrest.

Of course, The Trunk, in turn, draws its nourishment from The Roots, which in turn draws nourishment from The Soil—the same "nourishment of the last 12,500 years of the history of Britain" is available to every tree of The Great Arthurian Forrest—as such, it should be remembered that all Oaken Trees planted in the same soil each draw the same "Nourishment of The Soil" from it: therefore, it is not The Nourishment of The Soil that gives an Oaken Tree its stature, but The Trunk that supports The Branches of that Oaken Tree raising them to their preordained height over the Indigenous Forrest Floor.

Although one could easily be distracted by the matter that the same Nourishment of The Soil reaches The Branches from The Trunk as The Trunk had received from The Roots

240

which originally drew that 'Nourishment' from The Soil—and this is because every root of the whole Arthurian Forrest is capable of drawing its nourishment from the same "soil" of the last 12,500 years of The History of The Ascent of Arthurian Britain—the simple matter is that it is The Trunk of The Great Old British Oak that raises the stature of The Canopy of this special Oaken Tree so high over the rest of the forrest that everyone can easily see that this particular tree **has a different role** to the roles of **all of the other Oaken Trees** of the same Great Arthurian Forrest of Britain.

On the one hand—and despite the significance of its raised stature— The Great Old British Oak still remains an Oaken Tree—as such, its branches still represent a series of family pedigrees with a single pencenedl being senior amongst all of its branches: this is common to all of the Oaken Trees of The Great Arthurian Forrest—"an 'Oaken Tree is an

Oaken Tree', and it is the 'Arthur of Ravens' settled amongst its branches that not only protect that tree in the present but which ensures that it will get from one side of all adversity to the other".

Whenever you see an 'Arthur' of Ravens beating their wings around a Great Old Oak Tree, you should always thank God for his faithfulness to us and His mercy!

Yet if it wasn't for The Prophecy of Edward the Confessor's Deathbed Dream, it might seem paradoxical to realise that this tree has **Saxon** roots despite it being rooted in The Soil of Britain.

So, for the moment, we must take it as a matter of faith that each of the original Oaken Branches of The Great Old British Oak Tree must represent the pedigree of an Anglo-Saxon king who once ruled over an ancient Anglo-Saxon kingdom!

Picture, for a moment, an image of The Great Old British Oak standing tall, with its branches representing every king from when it was a young sapling during the early Anglo-Saxon invasions, representing every English king from those early days but including all of England's kings from that ancient era right down to the present day.

If it had not been that William the Conqueror cut down this Great Old British Oak in 1066, it would simply be a matter of charting all of the 'ninth-descent family tree branches' of every king that has ever existed since the tree first took root, right down to the present day—such an image might illustrate The Great Old British Oak in all its glory—but falsely so, as it turns out!

As it transpired, the story took a turn in 1066 AD when William the Conqueror cut down The Great Old British Oak, altering its historical trajectory—William was devoid of paternal Saxon roots, hence was not "of the tree", and nor was he of The Rheged Root—so from the time that the tree was cut down until some predestined time in the future when "green branches would be restored to the tree to flourish by their own accord", not a single princely pedigree **from William the Conqueror until the tree's predestined restoration** could be seen to be a branch of this Great Old British Oak.

We must, therefore, consider that this tree, once felled, could not grow new branches until a later date when new growth would again spring forth, doing so *as prophesied* in Edward the Confessor's Deathbed Dream.

According to Edward the Confessor's Deathbed Dream, this would be the time when '...green branches would reattach themselves to the roots of the tree and flourish by their own accord...'.

Naturally, when we interpret the dream itself in later chapters, we will be able to identify a specific year when the first of many new branches would reattach themselves to the root and flourish of their own accord.

Once we have this information, it will simply be a matter of adding every 'ninth-generation descent family tree' of every king of England that has existed since that date.

So, clearly, until we know of the date of the tree's restoration, we cannot 'for the moment in this chapter' attribute any 'king of England' since William the Conqueror as having a branch on The Great Old British Oak.

Of course, once we know the date of the tree's restoration—which would signal the reattachment of the family branches of any kings after this date—our charting of the tree will have to remain with its previous branches already sketched in, but

245

waiting for later 'reattachments' to be added to the chart of the tree so that we can then see it in all of its rejuvenated glory!

Therefore, until we finish examining the present series of Secret Cyphers, we will just have to be satisfied that we are able to recount the branches that existed **until** William the Conqueror cut down this Great Old British Oak in 1066!

The Branches of The Tree up until 1066

We need some sort of measure that we can use to decide which of the pedigrees of the early Anglo-Saxon kings can be attributed as branches of The Great Old British Oak and which cannot.

The following "Perambulation of the Stereotypical Oaken Forrest" uses 'the height of a tree' as a rightful measure that sorts these candidates into groups from which 'The Rightful Branches of The Tree' can be identified.

To view the respective heights of these trees, we merely need to stand back and view The Great Arthurian Forrest from afar—this will allow us to identify the different standardised **heights** of many of the Oaken Trees, which in doing so will allow us to broadly categorise them all ***by mere height***.

The first thing to do is to realise that despite the height of any of these trees, **all** of the Oaken Trees of The Great Arthurian Forrest are indeed "**oaken**"—that is, they each represent the family tree 'oaken pedigree' of a ninth-descent Pencenedl—that is, they represent the family tree pedigree of any ninth-descent family head whose line had been in Britain for more than nine generations.

With this in mind, we can stand back

from The Great Arthurian Forrest and ask ourselves what we see!

By way of an analogy, many readers will already be familiar with the modern-day "Cityscape" silhouette of our modern-day cities—yet here we are looking for the ancient "Forestscape" silhouette of The Great Arthurian Forest, where different ranks of Oaken Trees are categorised—hence identified—by height.

This will be a silhouette of The Great Arthurian Forrest that allows us to easily distinguish between the various heights of all of the various Oaken Trees that are collectively scattered across this "Great Oaken Forrest": this is the Arthurian way, this is how we categorise the various ranks of the forrest as can be characterised as being Arthurian.

So, having reaffirmed that an Oaken Tree represents the family tree 'oaken pedigree' of a ninth-descent

Pencenedl, then by recalling that we characterise **The Gathering** of all of these trees as being Arthurian, we are essentially reaffirming that the importance of the awen of what we are discussing is that anything that can be described as "Arthurian" is significant in that it is designed to **protect the heritage of our ancient ancestors**—which by having been called *Arthurian* has always had a trajectory of being passed from ancient days into the present.

Whilst realising that we are presently determining which ancient Anglo-Saxon High Kings had "standing"—that is, a "stature of height" that qualified them to be considered as being branches of The Great Old British Oak—the reason we are doing so is so that we can determine their significance in the context of Edward the Confessor's Deathbed Dream being fulfilled!

When standing back and considering the silhouette of the forestscape of The Great Arthurian Forrest, the first thing that we'd notice is that **the majority** of the Oaken Trees of The Great Arthurian Forrest are all the same height—which, in being so, causes us to realise that each tree of this oaken majority has the lowest regular height of all of the Oaken Trees of this Great Oaken Forrest: this Oaken Majority represents all of the lords of the forrest who are merely a Pencenedl because their ancestry has passed nine generations!

Although the Pencenedls of these trees have the **birthright** to sit in their respective Celtic Nation's House of Lords, they have not risen any higher—such as having been raised as a king over a particular Celtic National Council.

With this in mind, we can also see that some of the Oaken Trees of The Great Arthurian Forrest do have a stature that is higher than representing the 'mere majority' of these regular "Lords of The Ninth Descent".

Therefore, as we look over this vast forest from afar, we can see that there are various Oaken Trees of the same height that are taller than the rest and which, by large, represent the Oaken Kings of various Celtic Kingdoms.

Indeed, we can even see occasional intermediary trees that have heights that are between the heights of these Celtic Nation Oaken 'King Trees' and the lowest National Council Oaken 'Lord Trees' of these Celtic Nations.

These intermediary trees are essentially those trees that have been raised over the forrest under the authority of one particular National Council or another—such as to represent an Abbey whose hereditary Abbott represents the particular Oaken Pedigree which that particular tree extols.

However, having been raised by a particular National Council, these intermediary trees can never be as high as the Oaken Tree of that Celtic Nation's Oaken King!

Curiously, when standing and looking at the silhouette of The Great Arthurian Forrest from afar, one will also see contrasting heights between the heights of all of the various Oaken Kings—this is because the Celtic System allows for kingdoms to be divided amongst various heirs of a specific king, and various circumstances allow these new divisions to be administered as separate kingdoms—and yet the senior heir nevertheless retains the distinction of the seniority of his father, and because of this the various smaller kingdoms can be seen to represent **tiers of larger kingdoms that in turn scale upwards in rank** towards a prevailing High King.

As such, all of these kingdoms can be seen to be represented by a series of

Oaken Trees whose various heights represent the level of the tier that they represent.

However, our present task is not to map The Branches of any of these trees—but instead, to map The Branches of the tallest Oaken Tree in The Great Arthurian Forrest of Britain!

Quite obviously, the tallest tree of The Great Arthurian Forrest of Britain is The Great Old British Oak—and here, I'll reflect upon the etymology of the spelling of the word "forrest" (with a double-r) when applied to a forest that is an **Arthurian** Forrest: the double-r ('rr') spelling of the word forrest alludes to The Great Arthurian Forrest being *foremost* amongst forests, and here we can start to realise that it is the **height** of an Oaken Tree that distinguishes it as being *foremost* amongst all of the other Oaken Trees that are gathered around it— indeed, even the Pencenedl of every

Oaken Tree is considered to be *foremost* amongst the members of his own Oaken Family.

So, how do we start determining which Oaken Pedigrees qualify to be part of this Great Old British Oak?

With a little thought, the answer is obvious, and that's because we merely need to ask ourselves, "Which Oaken Pedigrees of all of the ancient Anglo-Saxon kings had ever been raised to **the greatest height** of the Great Arthurian Forrest?"

As a mere thought experiment, I'll discuss the first ten Anglo-Saxon High Kings of the Anglo-Saxon Heptarchy.

My reason for doing this is that we can consider them as **candidates** who might be rightly considered the pencenedl of their time who had managed to raise their own Oaken Pedigree to be a branch of the Great Old British Oak.

Without showing my hand so early, you'll remember from Chapter 4, "The Secret Cypher of The Roots", that the Anglo-Saxons started laying down their 'roots' in Britain around 449 AD.

The concept of a "High King" in Anglo-Saxon England is a bit ambiguous, as it doesn't correspond directly to a formal title or consistent succession.

However, in terms of dominant rulers **who had overlordship over other kingdoms**, a commonly referenced list is the one provided by the Anglo-Saxon Chronicle and other historical sources, which includes prominent kings who were recognised as Bretwaldas—Britain-rulers.

The **Bretwaldas**, according to the Anglo-Saxon Chronicle, are as follows, and these have generally been referred to as Anglo-Saxon High Kings—for example, Oswiu can be seen to be the 7th Anglo-Saxon High King in this list:

Anglo-Saxon High Kings (Bretwaldas)

- **1st**—Ælle of Sussex (488–c. 514)
- **2nd**—Ceawlin of Wessex (560–592, died 593)
- **3rd**—Æthelberht of Kent (590–616)
- **4th**—Rædwald of East Anglia (c. 600–around 624)
- **5th**—Edwin of Northumbria (616–633)
- **6th**—Oswald of Northumbria (633–642)
- **7th**—Oswiu of Northumbria (642–670), High King from 655
- **8th**—Egbert of Wessex (829–839)
- **9th**—Alfred of Wessex (871–899)
- **10th**—Æthelstan of Wessex (927–939)

We have previously discussed the Office of Anglo-Saxon High King as relating to the Anglo-Saxon "Heptarchy", which has effectively become a term of convenience because the actual number of kingdoms under the Anglo-Saxon High Kings fluctuated over time.

Broadly, if all of the Heptarchy of a particular age came under a particular king, he was a Bretwalda—an Anglo-Saxon High King—yet when a single kingdom of the Heptarchy broke away from the High King, he ceased being that High King, from which time the office of High King was in abatement.

The concept of Anglo-Saxon "High King" is more than a mere concept, it is underwritten by the process of the 'Overlords' of the Heptarchy having actually used the title of Bretwalda, and doing so in contexts that effectively made the office of High King part of the British Constitution.

It represents an actual office that legally prevailed, and the evidence of this is that later High Kings marched into various territories and claimed them by the rights of the office of a previous High King—for example, Edmund I marched into Cumberland in 945 AD and claimed it by the right of it having originally been articulated to the Office of the 6th Anglo-Saxon High King in 638 AD, then continuing to be so under the 7th Anglo-Saxon High King when he became the Bretwalda in 655 AD.

The circumstance of Cumberland having been articulated to England was down to the dynastic marriage of Rhiainfellt, Queen of Rheged, to Oswiu, the brother of the 6th Anglo-Saxon High King, but who later became the 7th Anglo-Saxon High King in his own right.

Oswiu further demonstrated his authority as the incumbent of the Office of Anglo-Saxon High King by commanding that every jurisdiction under his authority observed Easter by the calculations of the Roman Catholic Church instead of the calculations of the Celtic Church.

To many who know the finer details of Oswiu's history, this was a surprising outcome. That's because Oswiu had been brought up as a child in the Celtic tradition, later married two Celtic princesses, had a son of a Celtic princess who later became the Anglo-Saxon King of Deira, and had a daughter who later became the Anglo-Saxon Queen of Mercia.

This broadly illustrates that every branch of the Great Old British Oak inherited legacies from previous Anglo-Saxon High Kings, and the matter that Rheged is demonstrated as having been passed from High King to High King exemplifies the importance of our present undertaking to consider everything that we can glean from all of these Secret Cyphers being proven to be interleaved in support of each other.

With this in mind, I'll continue to chart those 'High Kings' who came after Æthelstan of Wessex in the previous table, who was tenth in that list.

Yet, continuing the 'High King' list after Æthelstan isn't so much challenging as it is academic.

We discussed in Chapter 5 how none of the Heptarchy ever again broke away from the Office of High King—hence, from then onwards, that office never went into abatement.

Instead, we merely need to consider that each King of England who came after Æthelstan was, in effect, the 'High King" of that which he prevailed over, yet as that office now had greater stability by virtue of not having break-away kingdoms, the High King started to style himself as "King of the English".

Then later, when geographical boundaries became better formalised, then instead of merely tracking "who" the King of the English prevailed over, he then became styled as "King of England", citing which "land" he prevailed over.

In Chapter 5, we also discussed how, for a few decades, the governing house alternated between the House of Wessex and the House of Denmark; in doing so, we considered that the propriety of the Danish king ruling as an "Anglo-Saxon High King" was **justified** merely because the Danish kings were also heirs of the Jutes.

That is, the Danish kings of England were the heirs of those who, along with the Angles, Saxons, Frisii, and Franks, had become commonly accepted under the name Anglo-Saxon—hence, they were included as rightful contestants of the Office of High King when their time came.

Although, as Danish kings, they also had their Kingdom of Denmark to rule, as *Kings of England*, they were effectively the new rulers of Jutland, whose house had been raised as Anglo-Saxon High Kings in England!

I'll continue from Æthelstan having been the 10th Bretwalda to those who followed him, who by the same token had been endowed with the same right to be considered a Branch of The Great Old British Oak.

Overlords

As demonstrated by Edward (959 - 975) *receiving oaths of allegiance from other kings,* the overlordship of all of these kings was effectively the endemic echo of the nature of overlordship being implied by they being a Bretwalda—a "Ruler of Britain".

- **11th**—Edmund I, King of the English (939 - 946)
- **12th**—Eadred, King of the English, (945 - 955)
- **13th**—Eadwig, King of England,

(955 - 959)

- **14th**—Edgar, King of England, (959 - 975)
- **15th**—Edward, King of the English, (975 - 978)
- **16th**—Æthelred, King of the English, (978 - 1013)

House of Denmark, 1013 - 1014

- **17th**—Sweyn, King of England for five weeks, (1013 - 1014)

House of Wessex (restored, first time), 1014–1016

- **18th**—Æthelred, 2nd reign, 1014 - 1016
- **19th**—Edmund Ironside, 1016

House of Denmark (restored), 1016 – 1042

- **20th**—Cnut, (1016 - 1035)
- **21st**—Harold Harefoot, (1035 - 1040)
- **22nd**—Harthacnut, (1040 - 1042)

House of Wessex (restored, second time), 1042–1066

- **23rd**—Edward the Confessor, (1042 - 1066)

House of Godwin (1066) Scions of Wessex

- **24th**—Harold Godwinson, (1066)

The Epoch of the Cutting Down of the Great Old British Oak Tree

William the Conqueror cut down the Great Old British Oak when he defeated Harold Godwinson at Hastings on the 14th of October, 1066.

Although the title of King of England was disputed by Edgar Ætheling of Wessex—who, with the support of the Witan, claimed the office between the 15th of October and the 17th of December 1066—his pedigree can't be considered to be a branch of The Great Old British Oak.

This is because The Great Old British Oak was cut down by William the Conqueror on the 14th of October—the day before Edgar's claim commenced—and because Edward the Confessor's Deathbed Dream is prophetic, no branches can be attributed to being on The Great Old British Oak after the date that the Conqueror felled the tree, and from that moment, right up until the tree would be restored in later centuries.

Although we will discuss the restoration of The Great Old British Oak in later chapters—indeed, we will identify a specific year in which it was restored—we should linger for a moment to consider the continuing "Legacy of Wessex".

The Legacy of Wessex

When William the Conqueror cut down the Great Old British Oak in 1066, the House of Wessex was on the throne of England.

The name "Wessex" means 'West Saxons' and pays tribute to the Saxons at large.

Naturally, it is no secret that when we discussed the Secret Cypher of "The Roots" in Chapter 4, we were already discussing the 'Root System' of 'The Tree' in the context that "The Trunk" itself connected to the predominant "Saxon Root", which itself was then connected to The Roots of the Angles, the Jutes, the Frisii and the Franks.

As already discussed, The Root System of The Great Old British Oak traced back to when the Anglo-Saxons started laying down their roots around 449 AD, doing so in the vacant Roman field that had been left empty when the Roman Empire started deteriorating in Britain around 388 AD, but which was formalised as being vacant when the Romans finally departed around 410 AD.

We shall, as we continue, assume the precept that 'The Crown' which King Charles wears today is essentially *in continuity* of The Wessex Crown, but in the context of The Wessex Root representing The Saxon Root.

Naturally, the final tally shall prove this, so let's join the dots between!

Thus, our task, from here on in, is to join-the-dots between William the Conqueror having felled the Great Old British Oak in 1066, and King Charles being 'The Wessex Heir' in this modern day—yet also discovering sometime between these two limits when "Green Branches" were restored to "The Root" that the Conqueror had left bare when he felled The Great Old British Oak, waiting for Edward the Confessor's Deathbed Dream to be fulfilled!

That, of course, will merely be another waypoint along the path of our quest, and this is because we need

267

to discover not just how the inter-leaving of those Arthurian symbols that are in the dream actually bear down upon qualifying the context of how Edward the Confessor's Death-bed Dream was always predestined to be fulfilled—but we also need to satisfy ourselves with a broad scope that once completed, would allow us to identify with certainty when the dream can be said to have been ful-filled.

The Legacy of The Branches

Although our immediate quest is to understand The Branches of The Great Old British Oak in the context that they represent the family tree branches of certain kings of England, we should also have due regard for the symbols of "The Branches" with respect to the generality of any fam-ily tree branch of any Oaken Family Tree.

In Chapter 2, we discussed the broad

subject of how kennings, circumlocutions, and Secret Cyphers were interrelated.

On the one hand, we discussed that the terms *kenning* and *circumlocution* were generally interchangeable.

Their common ground was that they were compound expressions with symbolic meanings. For example, *whale-road* was a kenning (or circumlocution) that meant *sea*. In this context, a Secret Cypher was merely a kenning (or circumlocution) whose meaning was still waiting to be rediscovered.

Yet there is a subtle difference between a kenning and a circumlocution, and this distinction is that circumlocutions are intended to convey meanings indirectly so that **the listener infers the meaning**.

The curious thing about this circumstance is that the craft of conducting one's speech so that **the listener infers the meaning** could well be said to be the crème de la crème of modern-day spy-craft: if a friendly force correctly infers the intended meaning of an expression of circumlocution, then its communication can be said to be successful—however if a non-friendly force intercepts a circumlocution and the sender is interrogated, the sender is well-placed to apply a different meaning to the circumlocution in his defence.

In covert operations, good circumlocutions always have plausible double entendres attached to them hence from the outset, the circumlocution itself **was already** a Secret Cypher:

- To an authorised recipient, the circumlocution would be capable of being properly decoded; yet,
- To an unauthorised recipient, the circumlocution would either seem innocuous or, at worst, have a high probability of not being able to be

decoded by an unauthorised soul.

The curious thing about Welsh Awen is that it is always attached to the tongues of our ancient bards and prophets, and this means that Awen—by its very nature—would always conform to the Four Great Prophecies of Arthurian Britain.

The exciting thing about this—in the context that one of those prophecies is about "The Red Dragon eventually rising to defeat The White Dragon, killing it in the process"—is that the built-in circumlocutive character of a Secret Cypher enables anything that you might **now** write 'off the cuff' to have its meaning *inferred by the recipient*, means that there is a built-in disconnect that prevents you from being able to be said to have sent any specific meaning that the recipient inferred: as such, the 'evangelical eagle' is strictly disconnected from 'the raven warrior'.

271

The reason that I'm mentioning this here in a chapter that is about "The Branches" of an Oaken Tree is that serendipity has afforded me an ephemeral opportunity to resolve a Secret Cypher that I first raised in my book *The Secret Cypher of Chalice Well,* but have not yet publicly resolved!

To wade into the prospect of resolving this, I'll start by asking the question:

• How are Secret Cyphers transported and delivered around The Great Arthurian Forrest?

Naturally, your first quest is to determine what this question actually means, and to aid you in this matter, I'm going to post the answer here, right before your very eyes!

However, I will post the answer *as a Secret Cypher,* from which you will have to **infer** *the answer* yourself!

The only two hints that I'll give you are:

1. Any reference to "branches" refers to "The Branches" of an "Oaken Tree" in The Great Arthurian Forrest!
2. An Oaken Tree infers a family that is headed by a Pencenedl of the ninth-descent.

Here's the answering circumlocution—think of it in terms of people:

Merlin to the Owl, to the Eagle, to the Raven ...

In the heart of the forrest, where shadows dance,
Merlin stood with his owl, in a mystic trance.
With a whisper of wind and a rustle of leaves,
He spoke to his companion, amongst the
   ancient eaves.

"O wise owl," Merlin said, his voice low and clear,
"Listen closely now, the secrets you shall hear.
For in the language of the wind and the tree,
Lies the wisdom of ages, for you and me."

The owl blinked solemnly, its eyes wide
   and bright,
As Merlin spoke of mysteries, hidden from sight.
With a flap of its wings, it took to the sky,

Harrison of The North of Branthwaite

Carrying Merlin's words, up high.

Through the branches it soared, with grace
    and might,
Guided by Merlin's wisdom, in the moon's
    soft light.
It reached the eagle, perched on a craggy peak,
And whispered Merlin's secrets, with mystique.

"O noble eagle," the owl spoke,
"Listen now, for Merlin's words evoke.
In the secrets of the forrest, lies the key,
To unlock the mysteries, for you and me".

The eagle nodded solemnly, its eyes keen
    and bright,
As the owl relayed Merlin's words, in the quiet
    of the night.
With a mighty flap of its wings, it took to
    the sky,
Carrying Merlin's wisdom, up high.

Through the clouds it soared, with strength
    and grace,
Guided by Merlin's wisdom, in the starry space.
It reached the raven, perched on a gnarled oak,
And whispered Merlin's secrets, in the
    forrest's cloak.

"O wise raven," the eagle spoke,
"Listen closely now, for Merlin's words invoke.
In the whispers of the wind and the rustle
    of leaves,
Lies the wisdom of ages, for you and me."

The raven cawed solemnly, its eyes sharp

and keen,
As the eagle relayed Merlin's words, in
the moon's soft sheen.
With a flutter of its wings, it took to the air,
Carrying Merlin's wisdom, everywhere.

And so, through the forrest, the secrets spread,
From Merlin to owl, to eagle, to raven's stead.
In the language of nature, they found the key,
To unlock the mysteries, for you and me.

You should have experienced some excitement, here, what!

There's an average of perhaps TEN Secret Cyphers *in each verse*—and yet there are ten verses!

What a catalogue of Secret Cyphers to consider—and this catalogue is made especially important because all of the Secret Cyphers should decode as circumlocutions about people, circumstances, and processes!

And did you notice that The Bear was not even mentioned?

Yet, **did you**, as the recipient, **infer**

that he was involved?

You already know from *The Four Great Prophecies of Arthurian Britain* that "Arthur will return as a raven", and on the one hand, a raven is mentioned in the poem, and yet on the other hand, ravens always get from one side of adversity to the other, who doing so *in Britain*, **always** beat their wings to the end of Arthurian interests.

Something that is *Arthurian*, of course, stands to defend the interests of Britain "as a bear would"—and we know that in Welsh, *arth* means bear!

Arthurian folklore is smitten with Secret Cyphers about bears, owls, eagles, ravens, moonlight, and even that double-edged sword of truth, *Excalibur*—and because of this, you should be able to follow how information is disseminated "in the Arthurian Forrest" from the previous poem.

Oaken Trees, of course, represent

individual family heads, and *The Branches* of Oaken Trees represent other members of the same patrilineal family tree: this is about the Arthurian community!

So, in the poem, when you read "through the forrest, the secrets spread, From Merlin to owl, to eagle, to raven's stead", what do you as the listener of this circumlocution surmise—what do **you** infer?

A "raven's stead" is, of course, a particular Branch of a particular Oaken Tree that he (the 'raven') happens to be sitting on at a particular point in time. Given that an 'Oaken Tree' represents the family tree of a Pencenedl, then this would imply that somebody who was personified as a 'raven-warrior' either belonged to that Pencenedl's family or was a trusted confidant of one of that Pencenedl's family members—who, in flying from oaken tree to oaken tree, was capable of spreading messages

277

from one trusted confidant to another, throughout the oaken forrest.

Although Arthur is not mentioned, doctrine passes from Merlin to The Owl, then The Owl passes wisdom to The Eagle, then The Eagle passes an evangelical message to The Raven, and then The Raven passes the secrets to which end he will beat his wings, from the stead of one branch, to another.

The curious thing about this is that no one role—that of the Sea-Hawk, Owl, Eagle, or Raven, told another role what to do—it was the **recipient** of "the whispers of the wind and the rustle of leaves" that received a circumlocution but in doing so, inferred the nature of what it would pass on to the next link in the chain, inferring it from the context **of its own** role.

I find this to be a particularly invigorating aspect of the Science of Secret Cyphers, and I followed up the previous poem with a triptych that expounds the individual roles of Owl, Eagle, and Raven; of course, the roles of Bear and 'Sea-Hawk' are well known!

Because I'd rather expound this further in a more appropriate setting, I'll not follow this triptych with a comment, but—just as I did in *The Secret Cypher of Chalice Well*—I'll leave it for you to resolve the reality of how this information might be distributed **by real people** of **designated roles**!

Curiously, the eagle might not even know that he is talking to a raven— that is, someone spreading an evangelical message might not know that a raven is the recipient of his message—and yet, the raven would infer his own message from the proclivity of his own role, then pass his own message to another 'raven stead'.

This triptych is as follows.

Harrison of The North of Branthwaite

"An Oaken Triptych"

I. Owl's Perspective

In the quiet of the night, beneath the
    moon's soft glow,
Merlin stood beside me, secrets poised to flow.
His voice, a whisper on the breeze, spoke of
    ancient lore,
Of mysteries hidden deep within the
    forrest's core.
With feathers ruffled, I listened, eyes wide
    and bright,
As he unveiled the wisdom veiled in
    shadowed light.
In the language of the wind, in the rustle
    of leaves,
Lies the knowledge of the ages, secrets
    none perceives.

With a flap of my wings, I soared into the sky,
Carrying Merlin's words, ascending ever high.
Through the ancient trees, I journeyed with
    a hush,
Guided by his wisdom, in the tranquil
    forrest's brush.

II. Eagle's Perspective

On the craggy peak, beneath the starry dome,
Merlin's secrets found me, far away from home.
The owl's whisper carried truths through
    cloud-kissed air,
Guiding me to mysteries beyond compare.
With eyes keen and sharp, I heeded
    Merlin's call,

The Secret Cypher of Edward The Confessor

As he unveiled the secrets that befall.
In the whispers of the forrest, in the silence
   of the night,
Lies the essence of existence, hidden from
   plain sight.

With a mighty flap of wings, I soared into
   the night,
Carrying Merlin's wisdom, boundless in
   my flight.
Through the endless skies, I soared with
   regal grace,
Guided by his teachings, in the vast
   celestial space.

III. Raven's Perspective

Upon the gnarled oak, amidst the forrest shade,
Merlin's secrets reached me, where I had
   long stayed.
The eagle's cry conveyed the truths concealed,
In the depths of nature's song, they were
   revealed.

With eyes sharp and keen, I listened to the tale,
Of mysteries whispered in the wind's soft wail.
In the rustle of the leaves, in the cawing of
   the crow,
Lies the wisdom of the ages, the truths we
   come to know.

With a flutter of my wings, I took to the skies,
Carrying Merlin's wisdom, as the night-time
   flies.
Through the moonlit woods, I soared
   without delay,

Harrison of The North of Branthwaite

Guided by his words, lighting up my way.

Thus, from Merlin to owl, to eagle, to
    raven's nest,
The secrets of the forrest spread, on nature's
    behest.
In the language of the wild, in whispers soft
    and low,
Lies the key to understanding, for all
    creatures to know!

Chapter Seven

The Secret Cypher of The Fruit

The implications of 'acorns' falling to 'take root' in "The Soil"

Two aspects of "The Fruit" would seem important to expound on. The first is how 'acorns', as "The Fruit" of an Oaken Tree, relate in general to any tree of the Great Arthurian Forest, and the second is how these relate in the context of Edward the Confessor's Deathbed Dream having been fulfilled.

We shall expound the generality of the first and weave the second into later chapters when we interpret the

Flesch—39; Reading time—19:17; Speaking time—37:05

dream itself.

"The Fruit" of an Oaken Tree

Considering the generality of "The Fruit" in relation to any Oaken Tree of The Great Arthurian Forrest, we must revisit the context where an Oaken Tree represents the family tree of a Pencenedl of the ninth descent.

In this context, an Oaken Tree represents a real person who leads his own family as well as having a seat by birthright in a Celtic Nation's governing council—its oaken 'House of Lords'.

In this sense, we must take it that "The Fruit" of an Oaken Tree—represented as acorns—are *kennings* that illustrate new Oaken Trees being seeded when an acorn falls from an Oaken Tree and takes root in The Soil.

You'll remember from Chapter Two

that a **kenning** is a compound expression with symbolic meaning—for example, we discussed the kenning *whale-road*, which means *sea*.

Here, we are trying to determine what the kenning of an *Oaken-Acorn*— representing *The Fruit of an Oaken Tree*—means!

Three kennings that illustrate this are interrelated: the *oaken-acorn, oaken-fruit,* and an *oaken-tree*.

Note that the word oaken has been used instead of mere *oak*: here, the impact of the suffix '-en' is to create an adjective out of a noun, and where the compound *oaken-tree* would be a tautology if merely intending to refer to an actual oak—if so, the expression *oak-tree* should have been used—here, it is the adjective oaken that implies that the intended meaning is broader than just specifying the tree as being a mere oak.

285

We've already discussed Oaken Trees at length, and the beauty of this kenning is that it can be used as a simple expression yet with the reader simultaneously visualising the complex idea of it representing a Pencenedl's family tree of the ninth descent.

These contexts can similarly be applied to *The Fruit* of an *Oaken Tree*, but instead, so that the reader can visualise the meaning of the kenning *oaken-acorn*—simplified as *The Fruit* (of the Oaken Tree)—so, we have to look a little deeper so that we know this kenning's intended meaning!

To explore this further, we must realise that 'when an acorn falls to the soil and takes root' so that a new Oaken Tree is formed, the metaphor implies that the new Oaken Tree would represent an actual Pencenedl who presided over the family tree members of that new Oaken Tree—so, because of this we must try to determine a sense of reality of what might actually be represented by this oaken-process of rooting an oaken-acorn in The Soil of The Great Arthurian Forrest.

It would help if you remembered that "The Soil" represents 12,500 years of the History of The Ascent of Arthurian Britain—we discussed this history in Chapter 3.

In short, the task at hand is to translate the symbolism embedded in the *oaken-acorn* kenning into the real-life visualisation that this kenning is intended to represent!

So, let's imagine that an arbitrary Oaken Tree has borne its "Fruit" in a particular season, that a particular 'acorn' fell to the "Forrest-Floor", that it 'took root' in "The Soil" of The Forrest, and became a new Oaken Tree.

We'll also be simplistic by imagining that a squirrel had somehow moved the acorn so that when the new Oak-en Tree grew, that it was not growing in the shade, under the canopy of the tree that dropped it as fruit, but that as such, this new Oaken Tree was growing so that its own branches would have an equal share of its canopy being exposed to the blue-sun-lit-sky as all of the other oaken-trees that were gathered in its vicinity.

The real question is, "What real-life process occurred so that the kenning of a new "Oaken Tree" grew that could be considered to have been a kenning of "The Fruit" of that original 'Oaken Tree'?"

It helps to remember that the indig-enous natives of The Great Arthurian Forrest who were beyond the ninth-descent were entitled to their share of land **by birthright**—and this was just as true for any come-of-age member of an oaken family, just as it was for that family's own Pencenedl. The ancient records of our forefathers illustrate that a Celtic nation distributed land to each Pencenedl and that each Pencenedl then distributed his family members their fair share.

This can be likened to a Scottish Clan in recent centuries, where the Clan Chief owned the land and then set each of his family members up with their own houses and farms, with access to forests, quarries, and other shared clan resources, etcetera.

So, with this in mind, we have to try and relate the symbol of 'an acorn falling from a tree and then taking root' to a realistic circumstance that reflects our Celtic history.

The most usual case of 'an acorn falling to take root' happened when an Oaken Tree's Pencenedl died so that, subsequently, his heir stood as the new Pencenedl in his place.

Naturally, the Pencenedl's heir who

replaced him would not be doing so as a new Oaken Tree, and indeed, quite to the contrary, he'd merely have graduated from heir-presumptive to Pencenedl in the same Oaken Family Tree, and who, as such, would have becomes the new family head of that same Oaken Family Tree.

Yet when a Pencenedl yields his position to his heir, the 'oaken tree' itself does indeed transform. It does indeed 'drop fruit'!

Oaken Family Trees trace back to that ancestor of their Pencenedl who represents his ninth descent—and although to qualify as an Oaken Family Tree, the family head must trace his ancestry beyond nine generations in a Celtic Nation, it must be remembered that if the ancestor of ninth descent was born in the Celtic Nation, then his father of the tenth descent of the current family head must have also been in the same Celtic Nation when his son of the ninth descent was born: as such, lineage beyond the ninth descent would have been achieved!

Given the precept that a Celtic family consists of all of the patrilineal descendants of the ancestor of direct ninth-level descent of the current family head, then technically, any **collateral** heir of that original father of the tenth descent that was through **his** brothers would no longer exist as part of this family head's immediate oaken family.

The curious thing about this is that in graduating to the tenth generation, the senior branch **descendant** of the **senior brother** of that original **father** of the incumbent of the ninth descent would have graduated to be a Pencenedl **in his own right**—giving birth to a new Oaken Family Tree!

This means that as a Pencenedl ages, it should already be known who the senior male member of his eighth collateral branch is: this person would therefore become a new Pencenedl in his own right the moment that original Pencenedl dies, and because of this, even the Celtic Nation's 'House of Lords' would have had prior notice that a new Pencenedl was on the verge of graduating as an Oaken Lord and would therefore soon qualifying to sit in that oaken 'House of Lords' by birthright.

In short, when an heir replaces a Pencenedl as the new head of a family, then that which was once the ninth-generation family tree root of the family graduates to being of the tenth generation from the new family head, and therefore the most *senior now ninth-level* **collateral** branch of that new family graduates to its own family tree head being a new Pencenedl who qualifies to sit in the nation's National Council under this new birthright.

In this way, every male **collateral**

branch of a Pencenedl will one day graduate to being beyond its ninth descent of its present Pencenedl, at which point that collateral family branch will qualify as being a new Oaken Tree which exists under the right of its new Pencenedl.

By the same tokens, the *first cousin* collateral branch of a Pencenedl would become the *second cousin* collateral branch of his heir, with existing *second cousin* collateral branches becoming *third cousin* collateral branches, and because of this, each numbered collateral branch of a Pencenedl increments by one when he is replaced by his heir—it's that process which pushes the existing eighth collateral branch **out** of the family when it becomes the ninth collateral branch—but which in doing so, creates a new Oaken Family Tree.

Yet this is where "Oaken Groves" form—although an eighth collateral branch is pushed out of the family when it becomes the ninth collateral branch, although it becomes an Oaken Tree in its own right, the new Pencenedl of that Oaken Tree is nevertheless still a junior part of the original descent from which it came, and as such, these new Oaken Trees that take root when each graduate from ninth to tenth, they collectively form the dynasty of an "Oaken Grove"— the gathering of all Oaken Trees who share a common male ancestor!

Although the big picture of this process might take a little while to understand, it is easy to realise that when the heir presumptive of a family head becomes the new Pencenedl upon his father's death, then every one of the direct line of his ancestors increases in depth: what was once the first generation in the father's line becomes the second generation in the ascending heir's line, and so forth—and where the previous line of the ninth descent changes to be of the tenth descent of the newly ascending heir, then the senior collateral heir of that ancestor who changed from the ninth to the tenth descent automatically graduated to representing a new Oaken Tree in his own right of similarly being of at least the ninth descent—thus adding a new Oaken Tree to their common Oaken Grove!

Although this is straightforward, we describe the manner of a collateral branch graduating to be a new Oaken Tree in its own right as though the original tree had dropped an acorn, which had taken root in the same soil, and grown into a new Oaken Tree in its own right.

In this sense, the acorn's crown represents the new "acorn-crown"—another kenning—of the new family tree. This 'acorn-crown' is worn by its family head, and as that family head qualifies as a Pencenedl and who as such has the **birthright** to sit in the same Celtic Nation's "House of Lords", then his new Oaken Family Tree will be seen as being gathered around the same Celtic Nation's Oaken "King Tree" which that House of Lords serves.

Yet this is only one way in which an 'acorn' may fall as "Fruit" from a particular Oaken Tree!

Keeping in mind that the Brythonic Celtic system comprises Pencenedls of the ninth descent, one must look at history and wonder how an institution such as an Abbey is set up in a Celtic kingdom.

In considering this, we must also consider that the Celtic system is designed to operate where Celtic nations are characteristically **oral**.

This gives us a hint as to why such things as Abbeys were set up under an office that prevailed as a Lord—in this case, an Abbott was set up as the Lord under which the Abbey was administered.

The curious thing about oral systems of governance is that they are typically not effectively governed by minutely detailed, wide-ranging constitutions: imagine an abbey being set up under an oral constitution that had every which-way of so-called *fine print* deciding how the Abbey was to be run—imagine what its Standard Operating Procedures were, etcetera! Who will remember the finer details of all of this in an oral system devoid of written documents?

It's an impossible task to run institutions in an oral system as though they were companies with bespoke written memorandums and written articles of associations!

For a start, the memorandum and articles of association would not be written down—and this is because it is the ethnic trait of Celts to conduct themselves orally—and this characteristic automatically dismisses the notion of such things as memorandums and articles of association being able to exist in an oral system.

The solution, of course, is to appoint a lord to prevail over the organisation—in this case, the Abbott would prevail over the Abbey as its Lord—under which its everyday operation would be managed by the Abbott, as well as by whichever officers he appointed into those offices that he created to assist him. This is, in essence, the origin of the modern-day term Landlord.

This brings us back to the mechanics of how such an institution would be set up. For a start, to be a Freeman of a Celtic Nation—which would hence qualify one to be a 'landlord'—one will have had to graduate beyond the ninth descent.

Crucially, one could only be allocated land as a freeman if one was at least of the ninth descent!

This brings us to a point where we can start interleaving our discussion with appropriate kennings.

So, imagine an Abbey being set up upon land that would come under the jurisdiction of the Abbott.

Here, the Abbott MUST be of the ninth descent. Otherwise, he could not operate as a Freeman of the land—without him being a Freeman, land couldn't be allocated to the Abbey, and this essentially requires that he be of the ninth descent.

This, in effect, requires that for any-one to be appointed a lord, such as if to preside over an abbey—or if even just a landlord—must be an individu-al who, belonging to an Oaken Fam-ily, is of at least the ninth descent himself. He need not be that Oaken Tree's Pencenedl; he just needs to belong to his Oaken Family.

This is where it becomes interesting: the nature of the Abbey being launched under an Abbott who is of the ninth descent means that his "Office of Abbott" can be described as an Oaken Tree!

Crucially, the moment an institution can be described as an Oaken Tree, *its commissioning* can be described as "the planting of an acorn"!

Naturally, this raises the question, "From what Oaken Tree did this acorn fall as Fruit?"

Only those who bear "Acorns" as "Fruit" can plant them to become "Oaken Trees; hence, the Abbey can only have been raised by an existing Pencenedl of The Great Arthurian Forrest.

This may simply have been a local Pencenedl raising the Abbey under his own right 'to sow an acorn'—who in doing so would most probably appoint one of his own family as its Abbott—either as a hereditary position or it reverting to his own gift in any circumstance that the Abbott ceased to fill that office. In this case, the Abbey would be part of his own 'Oaken Grove'—not to represent that it is his, but that it was being managed under the expertise that his family had acquired over the previous nine generations.

Another case might be the Celtic King of that Celtic Nation raising the Abbey in his mere right as a Pencenedl to do the same as a local lord might.

There are indeed many permutations of how such an institution might be raised—and of course, these need not be restricted to regular abbeys but instead be commissioned with the intent of becoming a special order, such as a university—but common to all of them would be the matter that it would have to be commissioned— that is, *it would have to be planted as if an acorn*—by a Pencenedl of an existing Family Oaken Tree.

It is in all of these senses that "The Fruit" of an "Oaken Tree" generates new life in "The Great Arthurian Forrest"!

Yet, having discussed all of this in relation to the mere genre of the Oaken Tree, how can we not discuss these in the specific terms of "The Great Old Oak of Britain"?

"The Fruit" of The Great Old British Oak

At first glance, The Fruit of The Great Old British Oak is just the same as The Fruit of any Oaken Tree. Whilst this is true, the matter that we see The Fruit of The Great Old British Oak in the context of it representing "The National Oaken Tree of Britain" then some of the behaviours exhibited by The Fruit of this Oaken Tree acquire a different profile than that which all other Oaken Trees are able to acquire.

For example, common to all Oaken Trees, including The Great Old British Oak, is the matter that its "Ruling Branch" represents a named Pencenedl, who, in addition to being "The Lord of The Oaken Tree", has a family that can be represented by a family tree of nine generations depth and breadth.

Yet, whereas ALL Oaken Trees exhibit this behaviour, the **visible profile** of every member of The Ruling Branch of The Great Old British Oak is *visibly raised* in front of the whole Great Arthurian Forrest of Britain!

Although we are yet to identify the specific year that "green branches" started reattaching themselves to the forlorn stump that was rendered bereft by William the Conqueror cutting down the Great Old British Oak in 1066, we can discuss this topic with the sure knowledge that since that year, the current branch of the Royal Family under King Charles is presently The Ruling Branch of a **restored** Great Old British Oak.

As to when green branches started reattaching themselves to the ancient root of the tree, we will have to wait until the next chapter to discover not only this but when Edward the Confessor's Deathbed Dream was actually fulfilled—and under what precepts.

Although a specific year can be identified that represents **when** green branches started reattaching themselves to the tree, *the fulfilment of the dream itself* would be when *sufficient branches were reattached to the tree* so that the tree could be considered flourishing.

And the deathbed dream even tells us what the mechanism is to identify under what conditions that that flourishing would assert that the dream had indeed crossed a particular epoch under which it could be considered fulfilled.

In the meantime, let's put the present Ruling Branch of The Great Old British Oak under the spotlight!

Given that The Great Old British Oak is an Oaken Tree—and in this respect, just like any other Oaken Tree—then we know that King Charles III is the tree's present **Pencenedl**.

From this, we can garnish that under "The Rules of The Great Arthurian Forrest", that Charles's **Oaken Family** must consist of every living person whose collateral branch on his family tree is of nine generations breadth or less.

- Before getting into the detail here, I'll first expound on the concept of comparing a family tree's generational depth with its collateral breadth: in short, eight collateral branches plus the branch of the Pencenedl equals nine branches breadth!

Firstly, the 'depth' of a common ancestor of a family tree **less one** corresponds directly with its collateral breadth—this is because the collateral branches of an Oaken Tree start with *the siblings* of *the heir* of a ninth-generation direct ancestor.

Naturally, the collateral branches do not include the directly descended Pencenedl and his children, grandchildren, or great-grandchildren, so although we count nine generations back to get **the root** of the ninth descent, **the collateral branches of the root** start eight generations back, so we add to that eighth-generation collateral branch the branch of the Pencenedl to get nine generations breadth!

I'll expound on this concept for the

sake of even further clarity!

Here, we are trying to describe a genealogical concept where the "depth" of a common ancestor less one—how many generations back the ancestor is—correlates with the "collateral breadth": the number of collateral branches, or side branches, descending from **the siblings** of *the descendants* of that ancestor.

Let's break it down:

1. **Depth of Common Ancestor**: This refers to how far back in the family tree a common ancestor is located. For example, a 4th-generation ancestor is four generations back from the present generation.
2. **Collateral Breadth**: This refers to the number of collateral branches stemming from **the siblings** of *the descendants* of a given **common** ancestor. A collateral branch is a branch of the family that is not directly in the line of descent but

comes from **the siblings** of **the descendants** of direct ancestors.

3. **Correlation Between Depth and Breadth**: This suggests that the depth of a direct ancestor in terms of the number of generations to him, less one, directly corresponds to the breadth of collateral branches—meaning, for example, that all branches from the siblings of the descendants of a 9th-generation ancestor with living heirs are considered part of the 8th collateral branch or less: here, you'll note that the 8th Collateral Branch plus the Pencenedl's own branch equals the nine branches that trace back to a ninth generation direct ancestor!

Therefore, **all family collateral branches** stem from **the siblings** of a **direct ancestor** at a specific generational depth **less one**, who are categorised with a collateral breadth that is equal to generational depth less one—for example, members of the 4th collateral branch are heirs of that direct ancestor who is five generations back, hence members of the 8th collateral branch are heirs of that direct ancestor who is nine generations back.

Notice that the heirs of a direct ancestor do not include the descendants of that direct ancestor's *siblings*—they are only through his own personal issue—that is, through his children!

This categorisation not only helps in organising and understanding genealogical relationships within a Pencenedl's family tree, but it also helps us define who, of a Pencenedl's deeper Family Tree that might go beyond nine generations, is part of the nine-generation depth of their "Oaken Family".

Here, I'll touch on King Charles III's Oaken Family Tree. Although naming every living member of The King's collateral branches up to the breadth of the ninth descent is beyond the scope of this book, we can glean some very interesting information by focussing on certain aspects of it!

First of all, the Family Tree of a Pencenedl is *patriarchal.* If it weren't, then identifying specific Oaken Family Trees would be virtually impossible.

A person can only be part of a single Oaken Family Tree; hence, the rules of descent need to qualify how one is attributed to which Oaken family tree.

This formula is both essential and far-reaching because it relates to how the birthright applies to those lords who are chosen to sit in a Celtic Nation's House of Lords.

This is the system by which Pencenedls are identified!

This means that his Oaken Family Tree consists of every male branch descendant of his ninth-generation direct ancestor, their wives, and all of their children—and indeed, all females who have not yet married or never did.

From this, we get a glimpse of the legacy of a bride being "given away" by her father—the bride is effectively being given away to become part of a new Oaken Family Tree.

For example, when Princess Charlotte is given away in marriage, unless she marries a distant cousin who is part of this same Oaken Tree, she will inevitably be marrying out of this Oaken Tree into another one.

Yet this does not mean that the bride who was given away is now unrelated to her original family; it merely means that, as a new member of her new husband's Oaken Family Tree, The Roots of both Oaken Trees have become intertwined.

So, for example, although King Charles's ancestry can be traced back nine generations through Queen Elizabeth II and through Queen Victoria to George III in that ninth generation, it is because this line passes through at least one non-patriarchal female line that quite clearly, George III cannot be considered to be part of King Charles's Oaken Family Tree.

However, it can be said that The Roots of King Charles's Oaken Family Tree are intertwined with the roots of George III's Oaken Family Tree, via they being intertwined with The Roots of Queen Victoria's Oaken Family Tree, via those roots being intertwined with The Roots of the Oaken Family Tree of Prince Phillip, who was Queen Elizabeth II's consort and husband.

Therefore, to find the living members of King Charles's Oaken Family Tree, we'd have to trace the direct male line back from King Charles but through Prince Phillip. Once we have found the direct male ancestor on that line to the depth of the ninth descent, it is quite easy to examine the descendants of that ninth descent direct ancestor and catalogue the living heirs of his male sibling's descendants to eight collateral branches wide.

In King Charles's case, his ninth-descent direct ancestor is Peter August Friedrich, Duke of Schleswig-Holstein-Sonderburg-Beck, who was born on the 7th of December, 1697, and died on the 22nd of March, 1775.

The House of Schleswig-Holstein-Sonderburg-Beck is a line of the Schleswig-Holstein-Sonderburg branch of the House of Oldenburg—and significantly, the House of Oldenburg, goes back to Widukind Duke of Saxony—a *Saxon Prince*—who died around 808 AD.

On an aside, this illustrates that one only has to trace one's own family tree back to around 1700 to represent nine generations—in King Charles's case, that went back to 1697; in my own case, it goes back to 1695.

From all of this, we can garnish quite a few things that are of tremendous curiosity!

First of all, if we keep tracing the paternal ancestry of Peter August Friedrich, Duke of Schleswig-Holstein-Sonderburg-Beck, back to time immemorial, we do come to a direct male ancestor of King Charles who was a Saxon prince.

We'll dwell on this fascinating revelation in the next chapter because it relates directly to the fulfilment of Edward the Confessor's Deathbed Dream!

Secondly, King Charles's **Oaken** Family Tree is rooted in the person of Peter August Friedrich, Duke of Schleswig-Holstein-Sonderburg-Beck. Because of that, every living person who is a direct descendant in the male line from him and who hasn't been given away in marriage to another Oaken Family Tree is part of King Charles's Arthurian family—his Oaken Family!

This gives a totally different perspective on how *the English Royal Family* and *the Arthurian Royal Family of Britain* are perceived.

Naturally, when Prince William succeeds Charles and becomes king, Charles's eighth collateral branch would become William's ninth collateral branch—which would not descend from William's ancestor of ninth descent but the one previous to it—hence, when William does succeed as heir, then on the one hand, the Oaken Family of The Great British Oak will be trimmed of Charles's present 8th collateral branch, yet at the same time new growth will be seen on the tree when Prince George and Prince Louis are married and have children.

For every collateral branch that is trimmed, a new one eventual- ly grows—for example, if the crown passes through Prince George, then the line through Prince Louis be- comes a new collateral branch, and if George and Louis had another broth- er or brothers, their descendants would be part of that same collateral branch because they would all have a common ancestor, Prince William.

What other 'fruit' can be gleaned from this? Well, although the oppor- tunities are vast—enough to write another book about—I'll illustrate an edge case to show how innovative some of them are.

King Charles's ancestry can broad- ly be described as German but more broadly includes former kings of

Greece and Denmark, and because of that, imagine Charles or one of his male-line descendants creating a special order of Abbey, then building some in various countries with Celtic heritage!

In doing so, under these Celtic precepts, an Abbott would have to be appointed over each Abbey who was already part of an existing Oaken Tree: thus, any of the living Oaken Family members of The Ruling Branch of The Great Old British Oak could be appointed as such an Abbott under Celtic Law, planting a new and genuine Oaken Tree in those countries, effectively extending the reach of the Great Arthurian Forrest!

This is not to say that Pencenedls of other Oaken Trees cannot do the same, because indeed, they can—but it does illustrate the magnitude of the opportunity for Celtic Revival with genuine ninth-generation heritage, right across Europe.

An illustration of the far-reaching power of a Pencenedl—keeping in mind that a Pencenedl has the birthright to sit in a Celtic Nation's House of Lords—is that Pencenedls have the right to issue passports that relate to people who are part of their own Oaken Family Tree, or connect with it in some capacity.

That's not to say that other countries are obligated to accept those passports; however, within his own Celtic Nation, the word of a Pencenedl is accepted as truthful unless he is judged by a court of his peers—a court of other Pencenedls—to no longer have this standing.

Chapter Eight

The Minutiae of The Dream

Resolving Edward the Confessor's Deathbed Dream of the Year 1066

Introducing The Minutiae

My working paraphrase of Edward the Confessor's Deathbed Dream is as follows:

- "In the Dream, two Benedictine Monks whom Edward had previously known in Normandy, came to him and pronounced that 'because of England's great sins, a great tree would be cut down, and at a distance of three furlongs, green branches would reattach themselves to the roots of the tree and flourish by their own accord'."

As discussed in previous chapters, this description contains various Arthurian *kennings*, which, until resolved, can be regarded as Secret Cyphers.

We have, in recent chapters, expounded many of the symbols of these kennings in the context that they were understood when the dream was first recorded by the then Archbishop of Canterbury—who, during that era, was an Archbishop of the Roman Catholic Church.

The significance of this connection with the Roman Catholic Church is that although the Office of Archbishop of Canterbury is now an Office of the Church of England—which would require an interpretation of the dream to be subject to the ecclesiastic due processes of the Church of England—it is because Edward the Confessor is also recognised as a saint by the Roman Catholic Church that an interpretation of the dream would also have to be subject to the ecclesiastic due processes of the Roman Catholic Church.

One would think that both churches would come up with the same result!

Yet, as an author, I am especially comforted because the Roman Catholic Church would also necessarily be involved in this—for those reasons I discussed in the Preface.

Naturally, the passage of the past, present, and future of Britain is subject to The Four Great Prophecies of Arthurian Britain—we discussed these from Page 90 onwards—and because of this, it is comforting that the Roman Catholic Church would effectively be standing as the "Gatekeeper" in this matter to prevent 'the ecclesiastical people' of the Church of England from being overly protective of the interests of the British State—instead of fulfilling their ecclesiastic duties to both God and the British people, no matter how the interpretation of the dream affects the British State.

That a "Gatekeeper" would be needed to hold 'the ecclesiastical people' of the Church of England to be diligent in their role is alarming, but as a Celtic author who errs on the side of safety, I'm quite uplifted that the general population is already equipped to understand the general seriousness of this matter.

This is exemplified by one of Nostradamus's quatrains, which is widely believed to apply to an era that starts around 2023 or 2024.

The greater issue here is not whether this quatrain is true but that a significant proportion of the population does believe it to be true.

On an aside, I do believe that it expresses truth, but it's not my place to promote that truth in this Children's Book, but instead, to resolve the truth of Edward the Confessor's Deathbed Dream.

The quatrain of Nostradamus that I'm referring to is as follows:

The river that tries the new Celtic heir
Will be in great discord with the Empire:
The young Prince through the ecclesiastical
  people
Will remove the sceptre of the crown of concord.

When I read this quatrain, I'm drawn to the third of the Four Great Prophecies of Arthurian Britain, which I'll reproduce here from page 91:

- The Red Dragon will be temporarily wounded by The White Dragon, but then The Red Dragon will rise and kill The White Dragon.

The significance of this is that the White Dragon represents the Anglo-Saxons, and when the prophecy is fulfilled, the essential outcome will be that the heritage of the Red Dragon—the Celtic heritage of we indigenous Britons—will be restored to Britain to replace those of the White Dragon.

Because of this, there will be a period before the White Dragon is dead when the British State will be naturally inclined to support the heritages of the Anglo-Saxons instead of the Celtic heritage of the indigenous people of this land.

In short, there will be a time when institutions such as the Church of England that naturally support the Anglo-Saxon State will be naturally inclined to err by supporting the White Dragon *when*, in all diligence, *they should merely be supporting God's holy truth of any matter*—which during this era, will be in support of the Red Dragon.

The Four Great Prophecies of Arthurian Britain have been accepted as true by the Celtic Church, and the amount of books that have been written in support of them can be measured in tens of yards of library shelf space—covering hundreds of years, and which fed by preceding oral disciplines, don't just go back to the Age of Arthur, but are rooted in the complete "Cycle of the Ascent of Arthurian Britain" that goes back 12,500 years to the melt of the last ice age.

This is why that quatrain of Nostradamus interests me—it clearly says that the 'ecclesiastical people' will support the Celtic position, and because of that, I'm edified to realise that the Roman Catholic Church is effectively set as the gatekeeper that ensures that the Church of England does a proper job.

If you haven't read this book's Preface, I encourage you to do so before proceeding!

Having brought to your attention that both churches have some due process to attend to that might take years—I originally wrote my interpretation of Edward the Confessor's Deathbed Dream at least 20 years ago—let's get down to the crux of interpreting it!

The dream itself was recorded in the Vita Ædwardi Regis, written in 1067—the year after Edward's death—and a copy of this in the British Library dates from around 1100.

As to what unpublished documents the Church of England and Roman Catholic Church might have in their vaults that are original first-hand accounts of the dream that were written in 1066—as well as first hand interpretations of it—only time will tell.

The following account of the Vita Ædwardi Regis is taken from a let-ter from Ambrose Lisle Phillips to the Earl of Shrewsbury in 1850—which by all accounts is very close to the original translation:

- "During the month of January, 1066, the holy King of England St. Edward the Confessor was confined to his bed by his last illness in his royal Westminster Palace. St. Ælred, Abbott of Rievaulx, in Yorkshire, relates that a short time before his happy death, this holy king was wrapt in ecstasy, when two pious Benedictine monks of Normandy, whom he had known in his youth, during his exile in that country, appeared to him, and revealed to him what was to happen to England in future centuries, and the cause of the terrible punishment. They said: 'The extreme corruption and wickedness of the English nation has provoked the just anger of God. When malice shall have reached the fullness of its measure, God will, in His wrath, send to the English people wicked spirits, who will punish and afflict them with great severity, by separating the green tree from its parent stem the length of three furlongs. But at last this same tree, through the compassionate mercy of God, and without any national (governmental) assistance, shall return to its original root, reflourish and bear abundant fruit.' After having heard these prophetic words, the saintly King Edward opened his eyes, returned to his senses, and the vision vanished. He immediately related all he had seen and heard to his virgin spouse, Edgitha, to Stigand, Archbishop of Canterbury, and to Harold, his successor to the throne, who were in his chamber praying around his bed."

Curiously, it was Harold, his successor to the throne and who was present when Edward the Confessor told the Archbishop of Canterbury about his dream, who was defeated by William the Conqueror at the Battle of Hastings later that very same year.

It is easy to imagine Harold's predicament, as heir to the throne of the dying king, hearing from The Confessor's very lips that "... God will, in His wrath, send to the English people wicked spirits, who will punish and afflict them with great severity...".

Imagine yourself as heir to the throne, thinking you will be a good king, yet hearing that wicked spirits will punish your people and afflict them with great severity!

What would have gone through Harold's mind when later that very same year as the new King of England, he heard that England was going to be attacked by the Norse in the northeast, who, having marched there and defeated them, suddenly had to turn around to march south on the news of William of Normandy having landed in Kent, who had come to claim the throne for himself?

Would Harold have seen it that he would survive?

To what degree of severity would his people be both punished and afflicted?

Did he foresee his own death, having heard that as a result of his people's great sin, that in addition to the great severity of punishment and affliction, that the prophecy of "separating the green tree from its parent stem the length of three furlongs" effectively pronounced that "The Great Tree would be cut down, but which would later be restored"?

To Harold, as King, he was the crowning glory of "The Green Tree"—what 'tree' was greater than he in all of England?

Surely, he would have considered that separating the green tree from its root would have cut him off at the crown's root!

And what counsel did the Roman Catholic Archbishop of Canterbury give him, who was present with him when Edward the Confessor told his gathered companions around the bed about what his dream had shown him?

It will be curious to see, as both the Church of England and Roman Catholic Churches go through their due processes of validating this in-terpretation of the dream, what an-cient correspondence from the then Archbishop of Canterbury that the Church of Rome has locked up in its ancient vaults!

If it exists, does the Church of Eng-land know about it?

Will the Roman Catholic Church sit on its hands until the Church of Eng-land reveals its hand, so that Rome can see if England's hand is in accord with any correspondence that Rome may have received from England in those ancient days?

We're fortunate because we can diligently expose the already-published dream to the stark light of truth.

We're essentially the third player in this adventure—we represent members of the Celtic Church—which is why I have gone into such depth about the Ascent of Arthurian Britain and introduced The Four Great Prophecies of Arthurian Britain.

The extraordinary truth is that the Celtic Church and the Roman Catholic Church already had a good working relationship in the first millennium, so much so that the Celtic Church submitted to King Oswiu's rulings in 664, at the Synod of Whitby, which were in favour of Rome.

Oswiu was not just the 7th Anglo-Sax-

on High King who effectively founded the Church of England at that
synod, he was also the king of the indigenous Kingdom of Rheged in his
right of having married Rhiainfellt,
the heiress Queen of Rheged, in 638,
but who had since died. As the king
of Celtic Rheged, Oswiu was deeply
engaged with the orbit of the Celtic
Church.

Oswiu's Celtic children of Queen Rhiainfellt would have still been in his
close orbit when he founded Whitby Abbey in 657 AD—the oldest, the
boy, became the King of Deira, and
his little sister became the Queen of
Mercia.

I have often thought that a garden should be established at Whitby Abbey in remembrance of these
two children of Rhiainfellt, Queen of
Rheged. It's very significant indeed
that Oswiu directed the abbey to be
built in the Celtic design, despite the
fact that he was the Anglo-Saxon

High King!

That is, the design of Whitby Abbey reflected the culture of the Celtic people of the Kingdom of Rheged, over whom Oswiu prevailed as King of Rheged.

Rhiainfellt, the mother of these Celtic children, was clearly the Princess Diana of her age, and there's little chance that she would have been forgotten when Whitby Abbey was created—which is directly due east of the Kingdom of Rheged—can you imagine that she was ever forgotten with two of her children in Oswiu's direct day-to-day orbit?

This shows how intertwined the Celtic and Anglo-Saxon roots were in those days, which in turn illustrates how strong the Celtic Church must have continued to be.

The Bewcastle Cross in Cumberland—part of the Kingdom of

Rheged—is believed to be the tomb-
stone of Oswiu and Rhiainfellt's son,
commemorating his Celtic roots at
the other end of his life. There's little
doubt that the Celtic Church would
have been involved in raising that
monument!

The sum of this is that the Celtic Church in Rheged submitted to
Oswiu's rulings at the Synod of Whitby, and as Oswiu could have ruled
the other way, it is demonstrated
that the relationship between the Roman Catholic Church and the Celtic Church was already "protestant"
in that evidently, *had Oswiu's ruling
gone the other way*, then the Roman
Catholic Church would have accommodated the Celtic Church's interest, instead of the other way around.

The reason "The Tripartite Relationship" between the Celtic Church,
the Roman Catholic Church, and the
Church of England is important is
that when "The Red Dragon" stands

proudly with "The White Dragon" dead at its feet, then the Celtic Church's significance in Britain will have been amplified back to its original strength.

Ravens always get from one side of adversity to the other, and with the victory of The Red Dragon over The White Dragon representing the full traversal from one side of adversity that started around 449 AD when the Anglo-Saxons first arrived in Britain, to the other side when the Red Dragon is finally the victor, the essence of the pre-449 AD Celtic Church will have been re-established in Britain with similar Celtic vigour.

This, in part, implies that the Church of England will undergo a Celtic transformation and that its relationship with the Roman Catholic Church will become as intimate as it was in the sixth and seventh centuries.

The very interesting thing is that the

Celtic Church and the Roman Catholic Church were always very good friends, and that's something that I put down to the matter that to the Celts, all manners of 'Protestantism' could be put down to being Brythonic Awen: that is, rather than expressing a legalistic sense of Protestantism, a Celt would be more likely to have accepted any ecclesiastic difficulties with Rome as merely being kennings that were representative of a figurative truth, instead of a literal truth.

Protestant Hardliners might be comforted by the witness of Christian missionaries in Muslim countries, where the wives of ministers typically walk behind their missionary husbands in public so as not to offend the Muslim community in which they preach.

Similarly, in the Jewish world, Christian missionaries often observe the Sabbath and adhere to similar Judaic legalisms to avoid offending the Jewish community exposed to their

337

evangelical outreach.

The more that you deal with Arthurian Secret Cyphers, the more likely you are to accept things as metaphors of a higher truth. For example, consider the following bible verses:

Matthew Chapter 13 Verses 34-35 (NIV)

34 Jesus spoke all these things to the crowd in parables; he did not say anything to them without using a parable.

35 So was fulfilled what was spoken through the prophet: "I will open my mouth in parables, I will utter things hidden since the creation of the world."

As a Christian Celt, this makes it easy for me to accept doctrines of the Roman Catholic Church that Protestants typically have difficulty with.

For example, as a Celtic member of the Church of England, I can accept the Roman Catholic position on Transubstantiation based on it being a **parable** that is presented to me as a **kenning**—a compound expression that I can decode into something acceptable to me.

That is, I can say, "It is **as though** the bread and wine have been transformed into the body and blood of Jesus Christ."

Here's the subtlety: If I treat this phrase as a kenning—"The Bread and wine is the blood and body of Christ"—then if a Roman Catholic Priest says to me "Do you believe that 'The Bread and wine is the blood and body of Christ?", I can also treat his question as a kenning, replying with a definitive "Yes!"

Yet that would not mean that I believe that the bread and wine had been transformed into the literal body and blood of Christ. If Christ spoke in parables, it is just as fitting that his priests also speak in parables—which, in this context, I can describe as kennings.

Similarly, if Christ spoke in parables, it is just as fitting that I would answer a priest's question in the context of it having been expressed as a parable—to answer a kenning with a kenning is one of the most fortunate forms of communication—and that's because it skirts around the prospect of any legalism being expressed.

Kennings don't contain the fine print that legalists thrive on!

A very good reason to hold this position is, of course, that not all gifts are handed out to everyone, so it is not reasonable to expect everyone to be equipped with the Gift of Discernment—the capacity to recognise stark truth—and the translation of parables between two parties in discussion gets around this paradox.

I will, for a moment, dwell on the matter that discernment is often expressed as "the ability to judge well", and although a glance at a dictionary will reveal the broader nature of this definition, it is worthwhile also dwelling on the word "judge", also the verb "to judge".

Judgement can be broken down into two components, *discernment* and *condemnation*—this is exemplified by most legal systems where the judge both receives the truth and, where needed, hands down a sentence of condemnation—so here, it is important to treat discernment from the perspective that stark truth is protracted, but done so without expressing condemnation.

This is why we should try to avoid conversations that are legalistic!

By way of example, if I am not equipped with the Gift of Discernment, then how can I categorically agree with the Roman Catholic Church's legalistic position on Transubstantiation? I can't.

Someone who offers an **opinion** is merely someone expressing a view **not** *backed by a Gift of Discernment*; it is quite astonishing that so many people take hardline views without having the Gift of Discernment who acknowledge this when they say they are expressing an opinion.

Yet, if I have not been given the Gift of Discernment—then it's not me who failed to receive this gift, but God, "The Gift-Giver", who chose to not give it to me.

In such a circumstance, why would I consider it important to offer a hardline opinion?

People who offer hardline opinions are essentially evangelists of their own inadequacies—in this case, trying to exercise a gift that they have not been given.

Yet, by the Grace of God, I can support the **kennings** that priests express as **parables** about an issue and, in doing so, accept them as **doctrine**.

I should think that if the Roman Catholic Church can accept the stance that those of its doctrines that Protestants typically have difficulties with can be accepted as mere kennings by its Celtic brothers and sisters, then I should think that a re-invigorated Celtic Church will get on very well with the Roman Catholic Church!

One even wonders that had the Anglo-Saxons not invaded Britain, there may not have been a Protestant Movement and its subsequent Reformation, *in Britain*: The Celtic Protestant Movement already existed in Britain as far back as 664 AD, and it would seem to me that the English suppression of Celtic Awen was the root of The Reformation in Britain in the first place!

The difference, in the final outcome

of The Reformation, was that Celtic Awen, in the form of kennings, were **marginalised**, **suppressed**, and **obfuscated**, and strict *legalisms* were applied that perhaps were never intended to be applied.

Naturally, further afield from Britain, this idea would presuppose the same outcome, had there been Celtic continuity across mainland Europe as well as here in Britain!

If this notion is true, then the mere "awenisation" of the Protestant Movement should effectively resolve the differences between the Roman Catholic and Protestant Movements, anyway.

Curiously, it's my view that one of the reasons that it has taken so long for the Red Dragon to stand up on its hind quarters to suffer upon the White Dragon its death-knell is the matter that Celtic Awen has, to degrees, been nationalised by the

Welsh, instead of being communicated in free-flowing measures, right across the Celtic world.

This is not presented as a criticism of the Welsh, who have indeed been triumphant in protecting the Brythonic heritages of the whole of Britain—not just those of Wales.

On the one hand, the Welsh have needed to protect awen as part of the broad Brythonic treasures that have been vested with them as custodians and protectors of our blessed heritage, yet on the other hand, the time has come for Celtic Awen to be taught to the wider Anglo-Saxon world.

You'll remember in the Preface that part of my Mission Statement is "To raise the profile of the **marginalised**, the **suppressed**, and the **obfuscated** heritage of Indigenous Britons and native Britain".

Well, in that context, the three children's books of which this book is the second in the series, attempts to start the reintroduction of Welsh Awen back into English and Scottish climes; from here, I would hope that Awen would be reintroduced to the British Commonwealth, The Americas; and in Europe, via the region of Tongeren as being The Centre of The Heart of The Celtic Triangle—that is, with The Celtic Triangle being from the north of Britain, to the south of Portugal, to the region of Galatia in Turkey, back to the north of Britain—which Awen would then be disseminated from The Heart of The Celtic Triangle, as though from the hub of a Celtic wheel back to all of Celtic Europe.

Where until now, awen has largely been marginalised, suppressed, and obfuscated, these three books make it impossible for people to discover the answers to the Secret Cyphers that are both presented and resolved in these books without emerging as "Learned Practitioners of Awen" alongside those who already do claim to be Celts—***all***, who by their very nature of being Celtic, ***are already standing on the threshold of being able to call themselves Awenydds***—pronounced "A-wen-iths", with the 'th' sound being vocally expressed as the vocal 'th' in the word 'they' and 'their'. Awenydd.

Introducing Two Methods to Resolve The Dream

There are two primary mechanisms to resolve Edward the Confessor's Deathbed Dream.

Both accept the generality of the dream representing "The Great Old British Oak" in the contexts already discussed—and this, in part, swings the spotlight around to the aim of discovering ***what year*** "green branches would start reattaching themselves to the root".

You'll soon discover that that year was 1714, the year that George I ascended the British Throne.

You'll also soon discover that the dream was fulfilled *in its first degree* in 2022 and that its fulfilment in its second degree is already underway in this year of 2024—but which may take years or even decades to complete.

As such, I would anticipate that this subject will eventually attain regular attention by the mainstream press and, in particular, attract much attention in connection with the subject taking always-reportable *incremental steps forward*—anyone who helps this subject attain that status will indeed deserve a favourable blessing!

The first of these two methods is called "The Ox and Plough" method, and the second method is called "The Patrilineal Heiress" method.

Both of these methods produce the same result, and for both, we need to combobulate the following Secret Cyphers:

1. "The Secret Cypher of The Distance of Three Furlongs";
2. "The Secret Cypher of Green Branches Reattaching Themselves to the Roots of The Great Old British Oak"; and,
3. "The Secret Cypher of The Great Old British Oak Flourishing by Its Own Accord".

The expression of these three separate Secret Cyphers reveals a very significant subtlety, and that is the matter of it illustrating that once we have identified *the specific year* that 'green branches'—the plural of three branches corresponding to three furlongs—were reattached to the roots of the tree', that although we can ascribe a sense of the dream's fulfilment in that **first degree**, we must also investigate the tree's subsequent *flourishing*, representing the dream's fulfilment in that **second degree**.

This, for example, would allow us to identify which monarch's ascension to the throne was in fulfilment of the dream, but also discuss the realm's subsequent flourishing as a consequence of that!

Before discussing any of these Secret Cyphers, I'll first state the real-world definition of what a furlong is.

Curiously, although the physical length of a furlong was always the same, how it is **described** varied according to when the question was asked!

What is Furlong?

The term **furlong** derives from the Anglo-Saxon words that mean *long furrow*. It was originally "how far an ox could plough before having to turn around and plough the other way".

We can, of course, apply some formally agreed measures and say that in the modern day, a furlong is 220 yards long.

This is because if we were to measure an ancient furlong, measuring the length of a long furrow to the point where the ox turned around to plough the other way, our modern measurement of 220 yards is what our modern tape measure would say.

Yet during the Anglo-Saxon period, what we would now regard as being 220 yards is actually 220 *new* yards— the Anglo-Saxon method would have measured us 200 *old* yards for the same physical distance!

There are three feet to a yard, and these *new* yards are based upon the *new* foot measure being only 12 inches long.

The Saxons used the "North German Foot" as their measure, which is 13.2 inches long, not 12 inches long.

The inch derives from the Roman unit called the Uncia—literally "a twelfth"—and a Roman inch was 1/12th of a Roman Foot.

The North German Foot was introduced to Britain, either by The Belgae Celts before the Romans arrived in Britain, or by the Anglo-Saxons after around 449 AD.

The important thing to remember here is that the **physical** length that an ox could plough before turning around remains unchanged—what has changed is the units of measure that we use to describe the unchanged physical length of a long furrow.

Therefore, both of the following measurements identify the same physical length of a furlong:

1. A furlong equals 220 *new* yards, which is 660 *new* feet, which is 7920 inches (where an English Foot is 12 inches long).
2. A furlong equals 200 *old* yards, which is 600 *old* feet, which is 7920 inches (where a North German Foot is 13.2 inches long).

You could equally describe these as English Yards and North German Yards, hence:

• A furlong is the distance that an ox can plough a long furrow before turning around to plough the field the other way, this corresponds to 7920 inches long, which corresponds to 200 North German Yards or 600 North German Feet, which corresponds to 220 English Yards or 660 English Feet.

In both cases, one just starts with a furlong being 7920 inches long, and for new feet (or English Feet), divide by twelve inches, and for old feet (or

North German Feet), divide by 13.2 inches. Then, just divide by three to convert old or new feet to old (North German) yards or new (English) yards, respectively.

In BOTH cases, the same physical length of a long furrow is described— these measurements are merely two descriptions of scale that we use to describe the **same** physical length.

These ultimately derive from the Anglo-Saxon fundamental measure of land, which was one rod.

An acre was 4 by 40 rods, and when ploughed, the long furrow was ploughed along the full length of the 40 rod side, hence equalled 40 rods.

This means that a furlong—a long furrow—became known to be a term that was interchangeable with the measurement of 40 rods.

Therefore, an acre was 4 rods times 1

furlong!

At the time, the Saxons used the North German Foot, hence a furlong became known to be 600 (old) feet long, and because 'there are three feet to a yard', this was equivalent to 200 (old) yards long.

Yet, in the 14th century, England changed to a shorter foot. Although the original proclamation was in Latin, it translates as:

- "It is ordained that 3 grains of barley dry and round do make an inch, 12 inches make 1 foot, 3 feet make 1 yard, 5 yards and a half make a perch, and 40 perches in length and 4 in breadth make an acre."

Curiously, the statement "40 perches in length and 4 in breadth make an acre" maps directly to the earlier measurement "4 by 40 rods makes an acre", and because a furlong was 40 rods, then a perch in the new legislation mapped to a rod in the original system.

The crux here is that the change from the North German Foot to the English Foot redefined the same physical length of a furlong to being 660 (new) feet long, which is 220 (new) yards long.

The Ox and Plough Method

This method focuses on the stark practicality of what a **furlong** represented to those who actually ploughed the fields of England when the dream occurred in 1066.

We derive this focus from that part of the dream that I have paraphrased as (once the tree was cut down, then:) "... *at a distance of* **three furlongs**, green branches would reattach themselves to the roots of the tree and flourish by their own accord".

Although we will still need to exam-

ine what the green branches were—
and *how*, at that distance of three
furlongs, *they actually reattached
themselves to the root of the tree*—we
should ask ourselves about how the
ox and plough "traversed three furlongs" when Edward the Confessor
had his deathbed dream!

In practical terms, the farmer drove
the ox and plough along the full
length of the first long furrow. The
farmer then turned the ox and plough
around and drove them along the full
length of the next long furrow. At the
end of this second long furrow, the
farmer once again turned the ox and
plough around and drove them along
the full length of the third long furrow.

Let's summarise this in terms of
broad, unnamed lengths: "There was
movement along one length, then a
turn, and there was movement along
another length, then a turn, then
there was movement along the full

third length".

- In short, the Ox and Plough Method describes "a length, a turn, a length, a turn, and a length".

Yet, why have I reduced the terminology to such bland terms?

Well—and here's the clever thing about Arthurian Awen—what I've done is to reduce the Ox and Plough Method down to two kennings:

1. The kenning of "A Length", and
2. The kenning of "A Turn".

The reason why this is useful is because it allows me to substitute some other kennings into this expression.

Here, I'm going to substitute the kenning "A Green Branch" for the kenning "A Length".

This gives us a new expression where the first of these can be seen as transposing to the second:

1. "a length, a turn, a length, a turn, and a length", transposes to
2. "a green branch, a turn, a green branch, a turn, and a green branch"

This is where it gets exciting, and that's because we already know what "A Branch" of an Oaken Tree is—it is *the Oaken Family Tree* of an Oaken Tree's Pencenedl.

As we already know that Edward the Confessor's Deathbed Dream is all about The Great Old British Oak, we must now regroup and compare what we are looking for—three instances of "A Green Branch"—with what we already know about The Great Old British Oak!

We discussed these branches in Chapter 6, "The Secret Cypher of The Branches".

Although "The Branches" of an Oaken Tree represent the family tree of that Oaken Tree's **Pencenedl**—which, as such, also applies to The Great Old British Oak—in the case of The Great Old British Oak, its Pencenedl is a **King of England**.

In Chapter 6, we were only able to trace "The Branches" of The Great Old British Oak up until William the Conqueror cut it down in 1066.

In that chapter, we deduced that the first "Branch" of The Great Old British Oak was the first Anglo-Saxon High King, Ælle of Sussex—that is, Ælle of the South Saxons.

Having traversed through all of the Bretwaldas, Kings of the English, and Kings of England, we were able to identify 24 Family Tree Branches on the Great Old British Oak, finishing with Harold Godwinson, who was defeated by William the Conqueror at the Battle of Hastings, in 1066.

Although we can't presently identify any Branches of The Great Old British Oak that are beyond 1066, we can, with a little supposition, make it our best endeavour to characterise what a later branch might look like.

We're not looking for a complete characterisation at this stage, but more for some little hints!

A characterisation that is obviously useful is that "The Trunk" of The Great Old British Oak connects to **The Saxon Root**, which *then* connects to the roots of the rest of the Heptarchy—the Jute, Angle, Frisian, and Frank roots—and, of course, to The Rheged Root.

This allows us to characterise the first 24 Branches of The Great Arthurian Oak as drawing nourishment from *The Saxon Root*.

Another thing that we can characterise is that William the Conqueror did not have patrilineal roots that go back to a Saxon Prince—and this leads us to want to examine every king since William the Conqueror and try to identify which ones had Saxon Roots.

We already know that King Charles III's family tree leads back to a Saxon Prince, so we can say that King Charles's "Branch" on The Great Old British Oak has "Saxon Roots".

We, therefore, want to try and find which other family trees of any king after William the Conqueror had patrilineal ancestry that can be said to be a "Branch that has Saxon Roots"—this is what we can suppose is a "Green Branch" that will reattach itself to "The Roots" of The Great Old British Oak.

Yet before doing that, let's return to our "kenning tree," which we suppose included "a green branch, a turn, a green branch, a turn, and a green branch."

So, let's imagine that The Great Old British Oak has 24 Branches, as already described—the last one was "The Branch" of Harold Godwinson, who was killed by William the Conqueror at the Battle of Hastings in 1066.

Let's *add* our "kenning branches" to that: in addition to those first 24 branches, we have "a green branch, (and somehow a turn), a green branch, (and somehow a turn), and a green branch", perhaps then followed by other branches—but finishing with King Charles's Branch.

The wonderful thing about this is that The Tree is now taking good shape—we merely need to identify which monarchs those additional branches belong to.

However, let's be a little transfixed on the newly added branches of the kennings—"a green branch, a turn, a green branch, a turn, and a green branch".

This is quite a scintillating expression, and that's because we know what "A Green Branch" is: its Pencenedl is a known King of England, therefore it represents his Family Tree—and we acknowledge that the Pencenedl's patriarchal line must go back to a Saxon Prince!

The immediate quandary, of course, is how can we present that "A King's Family Tree" (that goes back to a Saxon Prince), then "A Turn", "A King's Family Tree" (that goes back to a Saxon Prince), then "A Turn", then "A King's Family Tree" (that goes back to a Saxon Prince)?

The Family Tree branches are quite straight-forward, but supposing that we started a particular Branch at George I, how far would we go down the line of succession before we stopped at "A Turn" and then started a new Branch with the next King—and then, how far would we once again go down the line of succession before taking another "Turn"? And so on!

As it turns out, this is quite easy—let's look at the Line of Succession from King George I to King Charles III:

House of Hanover (1714 - 1901)

- King George I
- King George II
- King George III
- King George IV
- King William IV
- Queen Victoria (who married Prince Albert, from the House of Saxe-Coburg and Gotha)

Which brings us to the:

House of Saxe-Coburg and Gotha (1901 - 2022)

- King Edward VII
- King George V
- King Edward VIII
- King George VI
- Queen Elizabeth II (Who married Prince Philip, from the House of Schleswig-Holstein-Sonderburg-Glücksburg)

Which brings us to the:

House of Schleswig-Holstein-Sonderburg-Glücksburg (2022+)

- King Charles III
- (Heir Presumptive: Prince William)

The curious thing about this is that I've arranged these under the **Patrilineal** Houses of their male line.

This ignores the fact that on the 17th of July, 1917, by Royal Proclamation of George V, "Our House and Family *shall be* **styled** and known as the House and Family of Windsor".

This proclamation does not change the fact that the British House's "Patrilineal House" continued to be the House of Saxe-Coburg and Gotha until Queen Elizabeth's death, and that from Charles III, the "Patrilineal House" of the British Crown is the House of Schleswig-Holstein-Sonderburg-Glücksburg.

To accommodate the Royal Proclamation of George V, we can say, "The Patrilineal House that is presently on the British Throne is the House of Schleswig-Holstein-Sonderburg-Glücksburg, which by the Royal Proclamation of George V is styled and known as The House of Windsor".

This is the absolute truth!

The terminology House of Windsor is a mere style, and the truth remains that the House of Schleswig-Holstein-Sonderburg-Glücksburg is presently the **Patrilineal House** on the British Throne; the House of Windsor is **not** a Patrilineal House, per se, as demonstrated by it still existing since Queen Elizabeth's death.

Given this context, the "Branches" and "Turns" of the expression "a green branch, (and somehow a turn), a green branch, (and somehow a turn), and a green branch" are obvious!

That is, the First Green Branch in this depiction starts at King George I and "Turns" at Queen Victoria.

Here, the "Turn" is the mechanism where a female heiress married (in this case) a patrilineal Saxon Prince, which "Turns" from this Branch—this Patrilineal House—to the next Patrilineal House.

The Second Green Branch that was

"Turned-To" starts at King Edward VII and "Turns" at Queen Elizabeth II.

And the Third Green Branch that was "Turned-To" starts at King Charles III and shall continue to be the third Branch until the last in line of the Branch is a female. Naturally, the problematic thing here is that the new legislation that yields primogeniture to an older female in preference to the younger male is that the members of that Branch would still continue past that older female, despite the passage of the crown turning on the older female.

Also, each monarch was the Pencenedl of each Branch during their rule, but yielded that office to their heir when they died.

Yet the most important thing to note is that **all three** of these houses trace their **patrilineal roots** back to an ancient Saxon Prince—and in the process, the first Branch directly "Turned

To" the second Branch, which directly "Turned To" the third Branch.

Of course, the most curious thing is that since William the Conqueror cut down the Great Old British Oak in 1066, this pattern of "a green branch, a turn, a green branch, a turn, and a green branch" never appears elsewhere in the line of succession—hence we have proven the case of this pattern being directly contributory to fulfilling Edward the Confessor's Deathbed Dream!

In my own research, I can't find any king with male issue between William the Conqueror and George I who had patrilineal Saxon Roots, and because of this, we can say that the ascension of Charles III to the British Throne fulfils Edward the Confessor's Deathbed Dream in its first degree:

• Charles's ascension is three furlongs distant since William the Conqueror cut down the Great Old

British Oak in the year 1066!

Even had there been an occasional monarch with a patrilineal Saxon root between William the Conqueror and George I, the dream requires **three consecutive branches** *with* **Saxon Roots** for it to be fulfilled.

For the sake of completeness, I'll expound the three "Branches" and the "Turns" as follows.

First of all, I haven't found a single branch from William the Conqueror to Queen Anne—the latter, who preceded George I—which had surviving patrilineal Saxon Roots.

The First Branch—The House of Hanover—Turns on Prince Albert to The Next Branch

- King George I
- King George II
- King George III
- King George IV

- King William IV
- Queen Victoria (who married Prince Albert)

This first branch "Turned" to the next Branch because Queen Victoria, the last in the line of the House of Hanover, married a Saxon Prince—Prince Albert of the House of Saxe-Coburg and Gotha.

The Second Branch—The House of Saxe-Coburg and Gotha—Turns on Prince Phillip to The Next Branch

- King Edward VII
- King George V
- King Edward VIII
- King George VI
- Queen Elizabeth II (who married Prince Philip)

This second branch "Turned" to the next Branch because Queen Elizabeth, the last in the line of the House of Saxe-Coburg and Gotha, married a Saxon Prince—Prince Philip, a scion of the House of Schleswig-Holstein-Sonderburg-Glücksburg.

The Third Branch—The House of Schleswig-Holstein-Sonderburg-Glücksburg

- King Charles III
- (Heir Presumptive: Prince William)

Summary of The Ox and Plough Method

This method treats the kenning of "Three Furlongs" as representing the movement of an ox and plough over three "long furrows"—from which the name furlong derives—with the ox and plough turning at each end and then ploughing the next long furrow the other way, then repeating that pattern—to symbolically represent the family-tree branches of *three consecutive "Saxon Houses"* on the British Throne that "Turn" from one to the next at the last-in-line female heiress of that Branch.

Where the family tree of each house represents the 'ploughing of that dynasty in fertile soil' but which *turned to plough the other way* when a house's heiress Queen married a Saxon Prince—thus pre-qualifying the next house on the throne as being another Saxon House—then the matter that these "Branches" were Saxon Houses with Saxon Roots can be said to have symbolically "Reattached Three Green Branches (representing three furlongs) to the original Saxon Root of The Great Old British Oak".

In essence, the ascension of Charles III to the British Throne reattached the third consecutive Saxon Branch to the Great Old British Oak, which in doing so fulfilled Edward the Confessor's Deathbed Dream in its first degree.

We shall discuss the second degree of the dream's fulfilment in the next chapter.

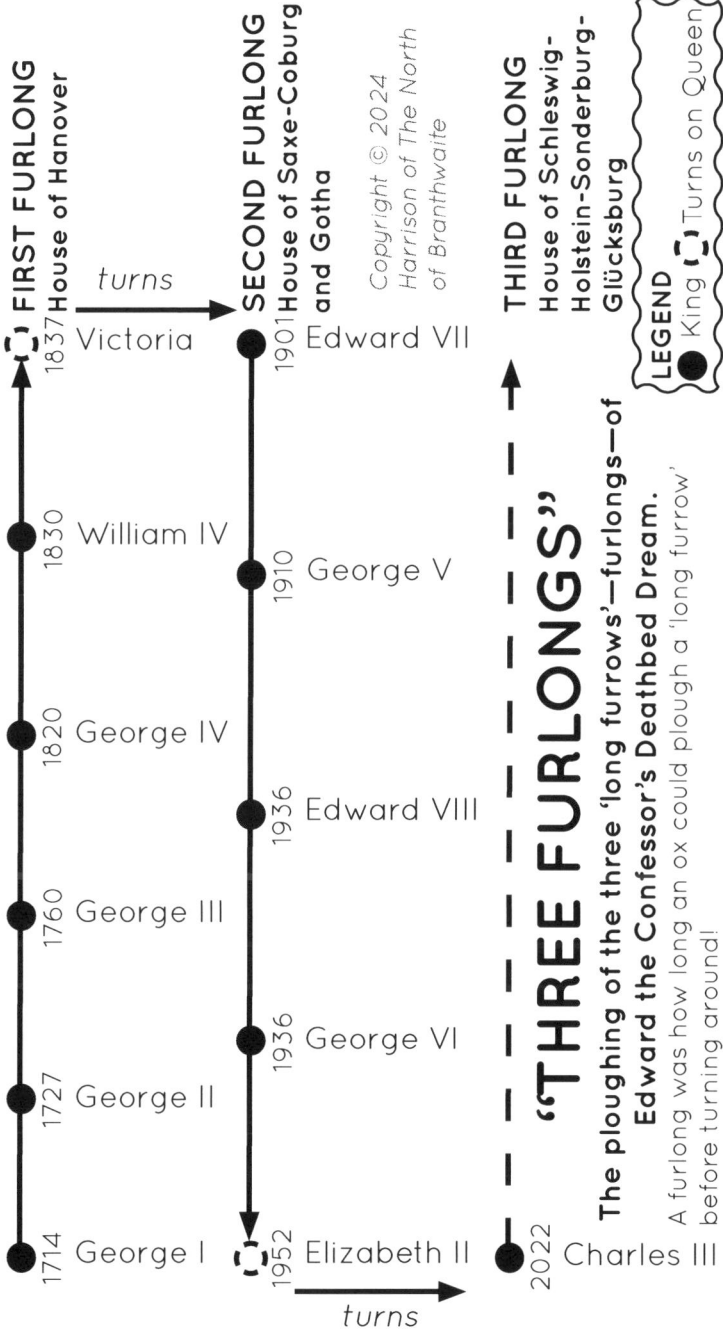

The Secret Cypher of Edward The Confessor

FIRST FURLONG House of Hanover

SECOND FURLONG House of Saxe-Coburg and Gotha

THIRD FURLONG House of Schleswig-Holstein-Sonderburg-Glücksburg

Copyright © 2024 Harrison of The North of Branthwaite

turns →

LEGEND
● King ⬚ Turns on Queen

First Furlong	Second Furlong
1837 Victoria ⬚	1901 Edward VII ●
1830 William IV ●	1910 George V ●
1820 George IV ●	1936 Edward VIII ●
1760 George III ●	1936 George VI ●
1727 George II ●	1952 Elizabeth II ⬚
1714 George I ●	2022 Charles III ●

turns →

"THREE FURLONGS"

The ploughing of the three 'long furrows'—furlongs—of Edward the Confessor's Deathbed Dream.

A furlong was how long an ox could plough a 'long furrow' before turning around!

The Patriarchal Heiress Method

This method is very interesting because, **in addition** to it actually *including* The Ox and Plough Method, it *also* flags the distance between Harold Godwinson—the Saxon king that William the Conqueror defeated—and George I, as symbolically being a **physical distance** of three furlongs.

That is, the three branches that The Ox and Plough Method identified continue to be expounded for the reasons discussed, but *in addition to these reasons*, the "distance" from the 14th of October 1066, when William the Conqueror cut down the Great Old British Oak, to the 1st of August 1714, when George I ascended the throne, can be said to be "Three Furlongs (of physical) Distance".

To shoot a quick flare into the night sky so that we are all visibly on track, we previously discussed a furlong equalling 200 old (North German) yards or 220 new (English) yards— so three furlongs would be 600 old yards or 660 new yards.

Let's suppose that a yard was equal to a year, using another process of kenning substitution! This was the basis of my first interpretation of the dream over 20 years ago!

Although William the Conqueror was crowned King of England on the 25th of December, 1066, he actually cut down The Great Old British Oak when he killed Harold Godwinson at the Battle of Hastings on the 14th of October, 1066.

The time span between the 14th of October, 1066, and the 1st of August, 1714, was 647 years, 9 months, and 19 days—including the end date.

Neither of these is either 600 "old years" or 660 "new years", despite being close—yet that is because the dream didn't say (paraphrased) "a great tree would be cut down, and at a distance of 600 (or 660) paces, green branches would … (etcetera)"—the dream said "a great tree would be cut down, and at a distance of **three furlongs**, green branches would … (etcetera)".

Here, it is quite sufficient to say that three furlongs is about 600 (or about 660) *years*—so, really, what the dream was asking was for us to look for the first new "Saxon Branch" (which is followed by two more Saxon Branches), somewhere near six hundred years after the tree was cut down in 1066.

So, if we do that—looking for new Saxon growth sometime after 600 years or before 660 years—when does it show up? The answer is in 1714, with George I's ascent.

The proof that this measure is suitable is because The Ox and Plough Method proves it—we do, from 1714, have "a branch, a turn, a branch, a turn, and a branch".

As demonstrated by the Ox and Plough Method, the first Branch started with George I in 1714. This Branch turned on Queen Victoria to become the second Branch with Edward VII in 1901, and this Branch turned on Queen Elizabeth II to become the third Branch with King Charles III in 2022.

Fulfilment By Degrees

Quite clearly, the third Branch was reattached to "The Saxon Root of The Great Old British Oak" in 2022, when King Charles III ascended the throne.

In that sense, one can say that Edward the Confessor's Deathbed Dream of the Year 1066 was fulfilled **in its first degree** when Charles III ascended the British Throne.

The third Branch is demonstrated already attached to The Great Old British Oak from that very moment the ox and plough turned the other way and started ploughing the third long furrow of the Family Tree Branch of King Charles III.

By English tradition, the then Charles, Prince of Wales, became King Charles the moment Queen Elizabeth II died—"The Queen is dead, long live The King!"—which, according to Queen Elizabeth II's Death Certificate, was 3:10 pm on the 8th of September, 2022—which is hence the exact time "The Third Branch" reattached itself to The Great Old British Oak.

I'd have thought that Her Majesty would have lived to be a hundred, and had I known that she wouldn't have, I'd have published this earlier!

This allows us to define a single furlong of the expression Three Furlongs, in Edward the Confessor's Deathbed Dream, as follows:

- **Furlong**: a *long furrow* in the context of the kenning "Three Furlongs" as mentioned in Edward the Confessor's Deathbed Dream, represents "A Family Tree Branch of a King of England which has Patrilineal descent from a Saxon Prince, *in the context of* **three** such branches being directly in a row where the last monarch of such a branch was female, but who married a prince who was already a patrilineal scion of a Saxon Prince."

That's true because when Charles ascended the throne, the "turning of the Ox and Plough from the second long furrow to the third long furrow" immediately reattached the third Saxon Branch to the Saxon Root that was originally left wanting when the Great Old British Oak was cut down in 1066.

We don't have to wait for the third long furrow to finish being ploughed before the dream is fulfilled in its first degree, and that's because the third long furrow—represented by the third Branch—is already reattached to the tree when the ox and plough have turned and just started ploughing the third long furrow: the green branches are already flourishing, and the ploughing of a complete long furrow merely represents the passage of every king of that house before the branch "turns" to a new branch.

The proof that only the first king of the third new Branch needs to ascend the throne for that Branch to be considered "reattached to the Saxon Root" is that only the first King of a new branch needs to ascend the throne for his new Branch to be considered reattached to that Saxon Root: the third Branch is equally "reattached", whether the first, second, or more, of the kings who will come of that Branch, who have ascended the throne.

Yet in Charles III's ascension having fulfilled the dream, you'll notice that I qualified that fulfilment as being "in the first degree".

I say that because there is indeed a second degree of the dream's fulfilment!

The Dream's Fulfilment in Both Degrees

The fact that the first degree of Edward the Confessor's Deathbed Dream has already been fulfilled is significant because it draws our attention to the full dynamics of God's plan for Britain.

Whereas The Four Great Prophecies of Arthurian Britain have a bearing on the second degree of the fulfilment of Edward the Confessor's Deathbed Dream, it is the fulfilment of the first degree that draws the attention of not just the peoples of Britain but also the nations of the whole world, to God's faithfulness to peoples who place their trust in Him.

Yet, to be specific, the fulfilment of the second degree gets its mandate from the part of the dream that expresses (paraphrased) "a great tree would be cut down, and at a distance of three furlongs, green branches would reattach themselves to the roots of the tree **and flourish by their own accord**'."

We will discuss this in the next chapter, "The Secret Cypher of The Great Old British Oak Flourishing by Its Own Accord"—abbreviated to "The Secret Cypher of The Flourishing".

REVIEW OF THE BRANCHES OF THE GREAT OLD BRITISH OAK

The following is a chronological list of the 36 reigns of all of the Royal

Pencenedls who have ever reigned as Oaken Family Heads of The Great Old British Oak.

To display these as "Oaken Branches", they would all have to be assessed in relation to their kin to determine which ones were part of the same 'patrilineal branch' to the ninth degree—for example, the 6th, and 7th Anglo-Saxon High Kings were both related in the male line, hence would be depicted in the same Branch, yet the 5th High King was not.

Similarly, the later individual "Houses" would prove to be the same Branch where their individual pencenedls were shown to be related in the male line.

Anglo-Saxon High Kings—Bretwaldas

- **1st**—Ælle of Sussex (488–c. 514)
- **2nd**—Ceawlin of Wessex (560–592, died 593)
- **3rd**—Æthelberht of Kent (590–

616)
- **4th**—Rædwald of East Anglia (c. 600–around 624)
- **5th**—Edwin of Northumbria (616–633)
- **6th**—Oswald of Northumbria (633–642)
- **7th**—Oswiu of Northumbria (642–670), High King from 655
- **8th**—Egbert of Wessex (829–839)
- **9th**—Alfred of Wessex (871–899)
- **10th**—Æthelstan of Wessex (927–939)

Kings of the English, and of England

- **11th**—Edmund I, King of the English (939-946)
- **12th**—Eadred, King of the English, (945-955)
- **13th**—Eadwig, King of England, (955-959)
- **14th**—Edgar, King of England, (959-975)
- **15th**—Edward, King of the English, (975-978)
- **16th**—Æthelred, King of the Eng-

lish, (978-1013)

House of Denmark, 1013-1014

- **17th**—Sweyn, King of England for five weeks, (1013-1014)

House of Wessex (restored, first time), 1014–1016

- **18th**—Æthelred, 2nd reign, (1014-1016)
- **19th**—Edmund Ironside (1016)

House of Denmark (restored), 1016-1042

- **20th**—Cnut, (1016-1035)
- **21st**—Harold Harefoot, (1035 1040)
- **22nd**—Harthacnut, (1040-1042)

House of Wessex (restored, second time), 1042–1066

- **23rd**—Edward the Confessor, (1042-1066)

House of Godwin (1066) Scions of Wessex

- **24th**—Harold Godwinson, (1066)

The House of Hanover (1714-1901)

- **25th**—King George I (1714-1727)
- **26th**—King George II (1727-1760)
- **27th**—King George III (1760-1820)
- **28th**—King George IV (1820-1830)
- **29th**—King William IV (1830-1837)
- **30th**—Queen Victoria (1837-1901)

The House of Saxe-Coburg and Gotha (1901-2022)—styled and known as Windsor from 1917

- **31st**—King Edward VII (1901-1910)
- **32nd**—King George V (1910-1936)
- **33rd**—King Edward VIII (1936)
- **34th**—King George VI (1936-1952)
- **35th**—Queen Elizabeth II (1952-2022)

The House fo Schleswig-Holstein-Sonderburg-Glücksburg (2022+)— styled and known as Windsor

- **36th**—King Charles III (2022+)
- ... (Heir Presumptive: Prince William)
- ...

As 'Saxon Princes'

The "Three Furlongs" of Edward the Confessor's Deathbed Dream represent the consecutive:

1. House of Hanover,
2. House of Saxe-Coburg and Gotha, and
3. House of Schleswig-Holstein-Sonderburg-Glücksburg.

All of these can broadly be said to be 'Saxon Houses'!

The House of Hanover is a cadet branch of the House of Brunswick-Lüneburg, which, as a principal part of historic Saxony, qualifies its rulers as 'Saxon Princes'.

The House of Saxe-Coburg and Gotha is a cadet branch of the *Saxon* House of Wettin, qualifying its rulers as 'Saxon Princes'.

The House of Schleswig-Holstein-Sonderburg-Glücksburg is a line of the Schleswig-Holstein-Sonderburg branch of the House of Oldenburg—and significantly, the House of Oldenburg goes back to Widukind Duke of Saxony—a Saxon Prince—who died around 808 AD.

Substantially, these three broadly 'Saxon Houses' can be considered to be "Branches" of the Great Old British Oak, which being consecutive, having "Turned-To" the next branch upon the last-in-line female heiress of the first two houses having married a Saxon Prince, can be said to have been figuratively represented by the expression "Three Furlongs" in Edward the Confessor's Deathbed Dream.

As a brief Colophon, it is interesting to note that Queen Anne—who immediately preceded George I in the first of these three branches—married Prince George of Denmark and Norway, who was from the House of Oldenburg: had Anne and George's child *Prince William, Duke of Gloucester,* survived into adulthood and succeeded to the throne, then the House of Oldenburg would have been established on the throne as a Patrilineal House, three centuries earlier than Charles III establishing the case in 2022.

This does, to a certain degree, underline the inevitability of Saxon Houses ascending the British throne and becoming immortalised as now defining the restored branches of The Great Old British Oak!

Visualising The Branches of The Great Old British Oak

Although I have previously repre-sented 36 kings as representing pen-cenedls of The Great Old British Oak, it should not be overlooked that this tree has had three growth phases:

1. The First 24 kings, up until William the Conqueror defeated Harold Godwinson at the Battle of Hast-ings on the 14th of October, 1066.
2. Not a single king representing a branch from when William the Conqueror cut down the Great Old British Oak in 1066 until the first branch was restored by George I in 1714.
3. The three branches of the House of Hanover, the House of Saxe-Co-burg and Gotha, and the House of Schleswig-Holstein-Sonder-burg-Glücksburg, starting at George I.

As such, when visualising The Great

Old British Oak in its **present** state, you should not visualise the branches of all 36 kings, as illustrated in the previous few pages; you should instead visualise just the Houses of Hanover, Saxe-Coburg and Gotha and Schleswig-Holstein-Sonderburg-Glücksburg as being branches that are ***presently*** growing on the Great Old British Oak—the previous ones were cut off in 1066!

To reinforce this, the Great Old British Oak looked like the following during each of the three major periods of its existence:

1. Up until the 14th of October, 1066—represented by the first 24 kings, as described earlier.
2. From William the Conqueror up until but not including George I—the tree was barren, having been cut off at the roots.
3. From George I until the present—the last three branches as described above.

Chapter Nine

The Secret Cypher of The Flourishing

The fulfilment of the dream in the second degree!

Introduction—The Significance of the Year 1066!

It is all very well saying that William the Conqueror cut down the Great Old British Oak *because the pattern of him defeating Harold Godwinson at the Battle of Hastings seems to 'fit the bill'*, yet wouldn't it be better that some sort of 'legalese' proved this to the nth degree?

As it turns out, there was such legalese, and that's because the changing of the King of England from one to another also involved the politics of the Roman Catholic Church, which eventually caused the change of one Archbishop of Canterbury to another.

This 'changing of the guard' is not only fascinating but also provides us with an authoritative view that conflates very well with the dream!

Although we can examine Edward the Confessor's Deathbed Dream from the perspective of it having been expressed in 1066, the **politics** of England's downfall began as far back as 1051, perhaps a little earlier.

Let's start looking at the version of the dream in the Vita Ædwardi Regis instead of merely looking at it from my broad paraphrase of it!

When the dream was expressed in 1066, it said, "The extreme corruption and wickedness of the English nation has provoked the just anger of God".

This means that at the time of the dream, the "extreme corruption and wickedness of the English nation" had **already** occurred, which had **already** "provoked the just anger of God".

This is a topic that perhaps a whole book could be written about—which I'll give some very illuminating examples about, a little later.

However, regarding changes that were to occur in the office of the Archbishop of Canterbury, Edward the Confessor had previously appointed a Norman cleric, Robert of Jumièges, as Archbishop of Canterbury in 1051.

To put this period of the Roman Catholic Church into context, the period of 1050 until 1080 is generally called The Gregorian Reform Period—it generally dealt with the moral independence of the clergy, but in doing so, also had some bearing on the Holy Roman Empire's claims, to which some interplay between the conflicting needs of both Church and State are evident.

The later Great Saxon Revolt was a civil war fought between 1077 and 1088 and which had its roots in the Saxon Rebellion of 1073-75—conspicuously, this included the Church breaking away from the clutches of the Holy Roman Empire, and this pattern of Church escaping from the clutches of European Statesmanship also appeared in England throughout the Gregorian Reform Period.

The curious thing about Robert of Jumièges, who was appointed Archbishop of Canterbury in 1051, is that this Archbishop became very involved in Edward the Confessor's adverse relationship with a powerful English earl named Godwin.

You'll notice that Godwin's son, Harold Godwinson, became The Confessor's heir, and it was Godwinson who was killed by William the Conqueror in 1066.

But let's rewind the calendar to 1042.

Earl Godwin had been one of the most powerful earls of England during the period when the House of Denmark was on the English throne—and in 1042 when Harthacnut died, Godwin supported Edward the Confessor's claim, which restored the throne of England to a "Saxon" royal house of Wessex.

Because of his power, Godwin even managed to secure the marriage of his daughter, Eadgyth, to Edward the Confessor. With this jewel in his crown, Godwin started building his own power base that became so prominent that it started excluding the king—upon which The Confessor, with the support of the Earl of North-umbria and Earl of Mercia, exiled Godwin from England in September of 1051.

Although Godwin was reconciled with the king the following year—partially because of his return in force—Godwin died of a sudden stroke in 1053. Yet curiously, these power plays had the unfortunate effect of drawing the Archbishop of Canterbury into the orbit of the struggle!

One of the ways of the world is that when the Archbishop of Canterbury makes a wrong move, the Pope gets a headache—and this was no mere headache!

As it turned out, Godwin—back in England in 1053 in even greater strength—had perceived that Archbishop Robert of Jumièges had influenced The Confessor to exile him the year before, in 1052.

The result was that Godwin influenced The Confessor to remove Robert as Archbishop of Canterbury and install Stigand in his place—and, of course, the state interfering in Church affairs was an affront to the papacy!

Significantly, Archbishop Stigand, who was the Archbishop of Canterbury when Edward the Confessor died, would have not just heard Edward conveying his deathbed dream to all of those who were gathered around his deathbed but who probably realised that the dream, in part, related to his appointment as Archbishop having been without the approval of the papacy—and which matter was still unresolved!

The most curious of these affairs occurred around the period when Robert of Jumièges had been deposed as Archbishop of Canterbury without the Pope's consent!

Pope Leo IX objected to the removal of Robert on the basis that Robert was still alive and that his removal had not been supported by a papal official.

The Pope summoned Archbishop Stigand to Rome on the basis of an appeal by Robert—Stigand failed to appear—the Pope excommunicated Stigand, but the excommunication was later overturned—yet Stigand was later excommunicated for a second time because he was acting as both the Archbishop of Winchester and the Archbishop of Canterbury at the same time, both which were the two wealthiest Sees in England.

Keep in mind that by the time Edward the Confessor was on his deathbed, Archbishop Stigand was supporting Harold Godwinson as The Confessor's heir—the son of the same Earl Godwin who had been instrumental in Stigand's appointment as Archbishop of Canterbury, those many years before!

You'd think that Edward the Confessor would have mulled over the corrupt nature of these circumstances on his deathbed—perhaps even to the point that through doing so, he was able to acquire such clarity in his dream when it came upon him in strength—but it wasn't The Confessor who provided us with the legalese that we are looking for to confirm that it was William the Conqueror who cut down the Great Old British Oak—it was the Pope himself!

On the one hand, it was Pope Alexander II, who was Pope in 1066, who restored the papacy as a major political force, yet on the other hand, he actively supported William the Conqueror's quest to acquire the English throne!

Born as Anselmo da Baggio, he had been elected to the papacy as Pope Alexander II in 1061, and it was this election whose precedence has stood for a thousand years since.

Prior to Alexander's election, popes were chosen by popular acclaim, which opened up the election process to abuses and influences by outside forces.

It had been Alexander's predecessor who had issued a papal bull that established the process by which Popes would be elected solely by the vote of a college of cardinals, and this set Alexander with a mission to reform the Church even further.

By 1066, the issue of Stigand having been appointed by the King of England without papal approval had caused the Church in Rome to find the need to discipline the kingdom of England. Because of this, Pope Alexander openly supported William of Normandy becoming King of England.

By 1066, William had completed his conquest of Brittany, and in seeking the Pope's support to invade England, the Pope gave William:

1. Papal authority to invade England;
2. A Papal Ring for William to wear so that he could demonstrate Papal Authority;
3. A Flag bearing the St George's Cross; and,
4. An official church document indicating that the English Clergy should heed William's reign once it was established.

William's part of this bargain was to allow the removal of Stigand as Archbishop of Canterbury and the appointment of one who had the approval of the papacy.

William supported Stigand's deposition in 1070, and the three reasons given for his being deposed were:

1. He held the bishoprics of Winchester and Canterbury at the same time;
2. He occupied Canterbury after

Robert of Jumièges fled, seizing Robert's pallium (papal authority) instead of seeking his own; and,
3. He received his own pallium from Benedict X, an anti-pope.

Broadly, it was **because of England's great sins** that the Pope himself had authorised William the Conqueror to punish England by effectively 'cutting down the Great Old British Oak'—and it was God himself, through two Norman Benedictine monks, who had told Edward the Confessor on his deathbed that the Tree that would be cut down, **would**, in time, **be restored**—which would then flourish!

When would this happen?

Well, according to the dream, this would happen **three furlongs** *removed from but rejoining* the Great Old British Oak having been cut down—and in the 'Age of The Confessor', this meant that *three "long furrows"* would need to be properly measured out and threaded together—so there'd need to be "a ploughing, a turn, a ploughing, a turn, and a ploughing" that made those three *individual* long furrows into a singular *collective* of three long furrows that was known as three furlongs.

This, we interpret as the first instance after 1066 when there would be three consecutive Saxon houses on the throne, where the first turned to the second, which turned to the third, threading all three together with the thread of Saxon singularity.

The second of these branches turned to the third on the 8th of September, 2022, when King Charles III ascended the British Throne.

The significance of this is that Edward the Confessor's Deathbed Dream extolled that there'd not be any growth of The Great Old British Oak between William the Conqueror and George I, that from George I, green branches would *start* reattaching themselves to the original Saxon Root, yet on the 8th of September, 2022, the third consecutive Saxon Branch would have **been reattached** to the Saxon Root, thus restoring The Great Old British Oak in the process.

It is in this sense that Edward the Confessor's Deathbed Dream was fulfilled by the ascension of Charles III to the British Throne on the 8th of September, 2022.

Yet this is only to say that Edward the Confessor's Deathbed Dream was fulfilled **in its first degree** by the ascension of Charles III to the British Throne on the 8th of September, 2022.

This is because the dream *also promised that a **flourishing** would follow* the reattachment of these Saxon Branches to The Great Old British Oak!

This flourishing would herald the fulfilment of Edward the Confessor's Deathbed Dream **in its second degree**.

But what will that look like? How scintillating will its portrait of truth be?

Rehanging 'The Portrait of Britain' in A New Frame

Although I've no doubt that a flourishing will follow the ascension of Charles III—the dream says so—and that this 'reflourishing' of The Great Old British Oak will be very wonderful indeed—we should first consider how properly interpreting Edward the Confessor's Deathbed Dream would tend to break the traditional frame of reference within which we tend to visualise the last thousand years of British history.

In realising this, we will effectively have to remove "The Portrait of Britain" from our 'national gallery', take it out of its old, now proven inappropriate frame, put it in a new now proven appropriate frame, then rehang it on a now white-washed wall of our 'national gallery'!

In this sense, historians worldwide now have the enormous task of rewriting the last thousand years of British history—reframing its context to one **that is sub-tended** by a proper interpretation of Edward the Confessor's Deathbed Dream!

Keeping in mind that The Great Old British Oak flourished up until the 14th of October, 1066, which was then dormant and without any branches until the ascension of George I on the 1st of August, 1714, and from then various branches *started* reattaching themselves to the Tree, *then nothing that happened in England between 1066 and 1714* can be attributed nor credited as belonging to 'The Great Old British Oak'.

In this sense, our familiar "Britannia,"

*robed, wearing a Corinthian helmet, and holding a trident and shield, was **sleeping** between 1066 and 1714, was merely **awakening** between 1714 and 2022, so nothing during that period can be attributed to her slate!*

It is in this sense that any accolade of this period that is traditionally seen as being a *British accolade* can effectively be denounced as actually not having been "of Britain" per se.

The justification for denouncing the credibility of this traditional 'British' status, despite the broad significance of the accolade on the worldwide stage, is clearly that it occurred *whilst The Great Old British Oak was without any green branches between 1066 and 1714, and which was effectively just an awakening infant between 1714 and 2022.*

Curiously, even though this concept forces us to *reframe* the historically accepted *traditional* points of reference of some of our visualisations about Britain and her nature as 'Britannia', this new perspective can indeed be of great value to us—I'll mention some of these benefits in a moment!

Yet, by the very same token, anything that has been attributed to Britain between 1066 and 2022 that is typically considered to have been adverse can also be reframed as not having been conducted by 'Britain', per se—which, as such, would allow "Britain" to avoid any responsibility for anything adverse that happened during that period.

Naturally, this means that we need to be careful about our language because although we can attribute any of these things between 1066 and 2022 to **England, The United Kingdom of Great Britain, or the United Kingdom of Great Britain and Northern Ireland**—depending upon the particular incantation of it during any particular age—the nature of **the fulfilment** of Edward the Confessor's Deathbed Dream effectively requires us to distinguish between England and both incantations of the UK just mentioned, **from** (indigenous) "Britain".

This will essentially be like the waters of 'The Red Sea' dividing so that a chosen people can walk between them. In the final outcome, the victors seen emerging on the other side will be we (indigenous) Britons of Britain.

This concept will grow as we progress through this chapter, so please bear with me!

In so far as where The Water of The Red Sea (of the Red Dragon!) started dividing, we should realise that although green branches started reattaching themselves to The Great Old British Oak in 1714, the fulfilment of the dream in its first degree did not occur until **three furlongs** had been achieved—according to the precepts of the previous chapter, 'three furlongs' would not be achieved until there'd have been "a branch, a turn, a branch, a turn, and a branch"—that is, from the moment the third green branch was reattached to The Great Old British Oak on the 8th of September, 2022, Britain now has a clean slate that is devoid of everything adverse that happened between 1066 and the ascension of King Charles III to the throne!

In this sense, the ascension of Charles to the throne was a full reset of Britain, perhaps likened to rebooting a computer where no new process or running thread existed prior to 3:10 pm on the 8th of September, 2022.

An arborist might say that The Great Old British Oak has been 're-rooted'!

At just first glance, this would make all conversations, such as about restitution for slavery, as now having nothing to do with "Britain" or "Britons" per se.

Here, the use of the words *Britain* and *Britons* is meant in its proper, indigenous sense—it does not refer to anything about the UK that, at best, could be described as British in the sense of the suffix -ish.

It will, of course, be of great relief to many people in Britain that finally, there is a just measure that substantially renders their need to defend themselves from "the sins of the fathers of our past" as now moot.

Although this might seem arbitrary, its better truth is revealed by considering that when the majority of the population of the United Kingdom eventually see themselves as heirs of the ancient Britons instead of as citizens of the United Kingdom, then a time will come when the threshold has been crossed where by large,

nothing adverse that happened between 1066 and 2022 will be able to be credited to we **native Britons—we Britons in our indigenous capacity—** but instead, should only be attributed to those who do remain citizens of the UK.

Naturally, I mean this in the sense of how the waters divide so that those who follow "The Red Dragon" can walk safely between those waters to the other side of adversity, thus fulfilling all of the Four Great Prophecies of Arthurian Britain!

Let's change from discussing this in abstract terms to discussing a few examples in rock-solid terms.

Let's look at two of the accolades that are typically attributed to Britain, yet occurred between 1066 and the ascension of King Charles.

Refuting the Significance of The Magna Carta

Perhaps the most significant, traditionally held 'accolade' that has had far-reaching significance in not just Great Britain, but by virtue of British colonisation, to most of the rest of the world, relates to those events that took place at Runnymede in 1215.

I'll first convey the traditional view of the Magna Carta, and then I'll refute it, positing that neither is it a British accolade nor something to behold as virtuous, but that the traditional view of holding it as an accolade actually works to obfuscate pre-existing, virtuous, *native Briton ideals of Britain.*

To start off with, the events that led up to King John being strong-armed by the barons of England in 1215 are traditionally held to be significant because they led to the sealing of the Magna Carta, a foundational document in the history of constitutional governance.

Here are the key points of its significance:

1. **Limitation of Royal Power**: The Magna Carta was one of the first documents to challenge the absolute power of the monarch. It established the principle that the king was subject to the law, not above it. King John of England was forced to agree to this document by a group of rebellious barons, marking a critical moment in the limitation of royal authority.
2. **Protection of Certain Rights**: The Magna Carta included clauses that protected the rights and privileges of the nobility and, to some extent, the common people. Key provisions included protection from illegal imprisonment (habeas corpus), access to swift justice, and limitations on feudal payments to the Crown.
3. **Foundation for Modern Legal Sys-**

tems: The Magna Carta influenced the development of common law and many constitutional documents, including the United States Constitution and the Bill of Rights. Its principles have had a lasting impact on the legal and political systems of many democratic countries.

4. **Symbol of Liberty and Justice**: Over the centuries, the Magna Carta has become a symbol of liberty and justice. It is often cited in legal arguments and political discourse as a foundational document supporting the rights and freedoms of individuals against arbitrary authority.

5. **Inspiration for Future Reforms**: The Magna Carta inspired subsequent legal and constitutional reforms. For example, the Petition of Right (1628) and the English Bill of Rights (1689) built upon the principles first established at Runnymede.

The Magna Carta's legacy is its enduring influence on the concept of the rule of law, the development of parliamentary democracy, and the protection of individual rights. It remains a cornerstone of legal and constitutional traditions around the world.

So that's the traditional view! And yet by large, everything just expressed already existed under the Celtic system that the Anglo-Saxons, in their spree of committing many great sins, had marginalised, suppressed, and obfuscated!

A more enlightened view reflects on the following part of the Vita Ædwardi Regis, which states:

- "The extreme corruption and wickedness of the English nation has provoked the just anger of God."

It is in the light of William the Conqueror having cut down the Great Old British Oak in 1066—who did so as God's instrument as part of God's remedial action plan against England—that even **the need for the Magna Carta** was evidence about 'The extreme corruption and wickedness of the English nation'.

Consider the following, which we started discussing in Chapter 3.

The Anglo-Saxons started their invasions of Britain around 449 AD, and as "Arthur" was immortalised as leading we Britons to defend ourselves against the invading Anglo-Saxons, we have to ask ourselves, "What was Arthur and his army of Britons fighting to protect?"

We can get some sense of answering this from the July 1860 issue of the Archaeologica Cambrensis, which states that:

- "A person passed the ninth descent formed a new pencenedl, or head of a family. Every family was represented by its elder, and these elders from every family were delegates to the national council."

Here, it becomes obvious that not only were we Britons already democratic, our Celtic kings did not have absolute power, they were subject to laws that were passed by that particular Celtic nation's National Assembly—its Celtic 'House of Lords', so to speak.

Quite clearly, the Magna Carta did not establish democracy in Britain, nor did it establish that the aristocracy and common people in Britain should have their individual rights protected.

As it turned out, one of the great sins of the Anglo-Saxons was to destroy the then pre-existing democratic systems and 'bills of rights' of the existing Celtic people of Britain.

At best, the Magna Carta was an attempt by the nobles to move some way towards restoring those democratic Celtic processes that already existed in Britain.

Naturally, we don't need the July 1860 issue of the Archaeologica Cambrensis to tell us that democracy was already developed in Britain—Caesar had already told us this when he wrote about these procedures being vested with the Druids, who he effectively depicts as an electoral college that had independent power to judge cases of legal significance.

In this sense, we can quite clearly recognise that the complete absence of branches on The Great Old British Oak between 1066 and 1714 allows us to **unattribute** the concept of the Magna Carta as having been the root source of democracy in Britain—and that does two things:

1. It forces us to examine our pre-1066 roots for any evidence of how

Indigenous Britons ordinarily governed themselves; and,

2. Given that we expect "Arthur to return as a raven", by which time "The Red Dragon will have killed the White Dragon", we can start visualising the native Briton heritage that we are able to revert to as part of Edward the Confessor's Deathbed Dream being fulfilled in its second degree.

Refuting the Significance of Henry VIII Making Himself the Head of The Church

Henry VIII's decision to make himself the Supreme Governor of the Church of England has traditionally been seen as having had profound and far-reaching consequences.

As with the previous section, I'll expound the traditional view, and then I'll refute it on the basis that Henry VIII's actions occurred during that period of the Great Old British Oak's life when it didn't have any branches on that Tree—that is, between 1066 and 1714.

Then, I'll similarly go on to say that the Celtic Church was already Protestant in these matters, and that in fact Henry VIII's actions were detrimental to the pre-existing Celtic position, which, by large, already extolled both its freedom **from** Rome, yet companionship **with** Rome.

Here are the key points of its *traditionally* viewed significance:

Religious Significance

1. **Break with the Roman Catholic Church**: By declaring himself the Supreme Head of the Church of England through the Act of Supremacy in 1534, Henry VIII effectively broke away from the authority of the Pope and the Roman Catholic Church. This marked the beginning of the English Reforma-

tion.

2. **Formation of the Church of England**: This move led to the establishment of the Church of England, with the monarch as its head. It created a national church that was independent of papal authority.

3. **Religious Reforms**: Henry VIII initiated a series of religious reforms, including the dissolution of monasteries and the redistribution of their wealth and lands. These reforms led to significant changes in the religious landscape of England.

Political Significance

1. **Consolidation of Power**: By assuming control over the Church, Henry VIII consolidated his political power. He eliminated the influence of the Pope in English affairs and asserted his sovereignty over religious matters.

2. **Economic Gains**: The dissolution of monasteries and the seizure of church lands and wealth sig-

nificantly increased the crown's revenues. This helped to finance Henry's government and military campaigns.

3. **Control Over Religious Practices**: As the head of the Church, Henry VIII could dictate religious practices and doctrines within his realm. This allowed him to enforce religious uniformity and reduce dissent.

Social and Cultural Significance

1. **Impact on Clergy and Monastic Life**: The dissolution of monasteries led to the displacement of monks and nuns and the loss of a significant part of the social welfare system that monasteries provided, such as education and care for the poor.

2. **Long-term Religious Conflict**: Henry VIII's actions set the stage for ongoing religious conflict in England. His successors, particularly under the reigns of his children

Edward VI, Mary I, and Elizabeth I, continued to face significant religious turmoil and persecution based on shifting policies between Protestantism and Catholicism.

3. **Cultural Shift**: The break with Rome and the subsequent religious reforms contributed to the spread of Renaissance humanism and new theological ideas within England. It also laid the groundwork for future developments in English religious and cultural identity.

Legal and Constitutional Significance

1. **Precedent for Royal Supremacy**: The Act of Supremacy and related legislation established a legal precedent for the monarch's supremacy over the Church. This concept of royal supremacy would influence English constitutional development and the relationship between Church and State.

2. **Foundation for Future Religious**

Legislation: Henry VIII's establishment of the Church of England created a framework for future religious legislation and reform. This included the development of Anglican doctrine and liturgy, which would be formalised in subsequent reigns.

In summary, the traditional view of Henry VIII making himself the Supreme Governor of the Church had profound religious, political, social, cultural, legal, and constitutional implications, fundamentally altering the trajectory of English history.

Refuting the Significance of Henry VIII's Reforms

As with the previous section, we can consider Henry VIII's actions an attempt to redress the situation created by "the extreme corruption and wickedness of the English nation."

Naturally, some of his actions—compared to the previous Celtic position—also appear misguided!

Although Edward the Confessor is traditionally viewed as being the only one of England's saints to have been made a saint by both the Church of England and the Roman Catholic Church, this position is quite misleading.

The reason why it can be misleading is that the birthplace of the Church of England is often held to have been the Synod of Whitby, which was convened in the year 664 AD by Oswiu, the 7th Anglo-Saxon High King.

Yet Oswiu, his older brother Oswald, and Edwin, the previous king—all Anglo-Saxon High Kings, the 7th, 6th, and 5th, respectively—were also recognised as saints of the Church.

This means that after the Church of England's "birth" at the Synod of Whitby, then all three of Oswiu, his brother Oswald, and Edwin, can be said to be saints of the Church of England, as well as saints of the Roman Catholic Church, *in addition* to Edward the Confessor.

This realisation allows us to follow the attrition of 'The English Church' from its time in harmony with the Celtic Church around 664 AD, to Edward the Confessor, and then to Henry VIII.

Curiously, Oswiu had been brought up in the traditions of the Celtic Church, and when he commissioned Whitby Abbey to be built in 657 AD, he commissioned it to be built in the Celtic design.

Similarly, the decisions that Oswiu made at the Synod of Whitby were only made to be observed in those jurisdictions that Oswiu prevailed over—both Celtic and Anglo-Saxon—this is proven by the matter that when Oswiu made his monumental decisions at Whitby, Colmán, the

Bishop of Lindisfarne, and others, re-signed their positions in protest and returned to Iona—which was not in the geographical precinct of Oswiu's jurisdiction.

Hence, *Colmán et al* needed not ob-serve Oswiu's rulings of The Synod, having travelled outside of Oswiu's geographical jurisdiction to Iona.

Yet, to the contrary, everyone with-in Oswiu's geographic jurisdiction needed to submit to his rulings of The Synod—broadly, those in the King-dom of Rheged and those in all of the Anglo-Saxon kingdoms that Oswiu had prevailed over as Anglo-Saxon High King since 655 AD, were sub-ject to his rulings made at the Synod of Whitby.

Here, it matters not so much that Oswiu was the Anglo-Saxon High King but that in both his Celtic and Anglo-Saxon jurisdictions, all of the churches were subservient to the rulings he made at the synod.

As such, that made Oswiu, **in his separate capacities** of King of Rheged and Anglo-Saxon High King, the Administrative Head of the Celtic Church and the Administrative Head of the Roman Catholic 'Church of England', *in those geographic jurisdictions*, respectively.

This illustrates that in 664 AD, the Roman Catholic Church and the Celtic Church already had a good relationship and that the Celtic Church had sufficient capability to be regarded as 'Protestant of Rome' when it needed to make its own rulings but also 'Companion of Rome' in all other matters.

Naturally, this did not make Oswiu the evangelical head of any of these churches, and this is exemplified today in the matter that in England, despite that Charles III is The Supreme Governor of the Church of England, evangelical matters are vested in the Archbishop of Canterbury—but not in His Grace's office of Archbishop, instead, in His Grace's capacity as Primate of All England; similarly, in The North, evangelical matters are vested in the Archbishop of York in His Grace's capacity as Primate of England!

Thus, if we compare Oswiu's position as the effective "Supreme Governor of the Celtic Church in the Kingdom of Rheged," there is little difference between that 7th-century position and today's position—Oswiu was already the effective 'Supreme Governor' of the Roman Catholic 'Church of England', as well as the effective 'Supreme Governor' of the Celtic Church.

This illustrates that Henry VIII's actions were essentially needed to redress the Anglo-Saxon attrition of the Celtic position, which had already occurred prior to 1066.

The important thing to consider here is that by 'closing the window of history' between 1066 and 2022, we can look at all of the Anglo-Saxon accolades created during that period. However, in looking back before 1066, we generally find them already existing in the Celtic system, but in a better Celtic context.

Resolving the Secret Cypher of The Flourishing

Once again, I'll start looking at the version of the dream in the Vita Ædwardi Regis instead of merely looking at it from my broad paraphrase of it!

The parts that I wish to dwell on illustrate how the fulfilment of Edward the Confessor's Deathbed Dream can be separated into two degrees, "Fulfilment in the First Degree" and "Fulfilment in the Second Degree".

1. **Fulfilment in its first degree**: "When

malice shall have reached the fullness of its measure, God will, in His wrath, send to the English people wicked spirits, who will punish and afflict them with great severity, by separating the green tree from its parent stem the length of three furlongs."

2. **Fulfilment in its second degree**: "But at last, this same tree, through the compassionate mercy of God, and without any national (governmental) assistance, shall return to its original root, reflourish, and bear abundant fruit."

Although these two statements run together as part of the single original statement of the Vita Ædwardi Regis, there is a distinct 'turning' from the fulfilment in the first degree, to fulfilment in the second degree, which pivots on the statement "But at last, this same tree, ...".

Immediately before this term, the text had already said, "...by separating the green tree from its parent stem the length of three furlongs"—and the significance of this is that the text had **already** identified the "... separating of the green tree *from its parent stem* **the length of three furlongs**".

Significantly, the first degree is already defined by this statement—if a second degree was not intended, then the statement would not need the rest of the text that follows the statement "But at last, this same tree, ...".

Just to clarify this, if we use the hermeneutics that we applied in previous chapters to the phrase "by separating the green tree from its parent stem the length of three furlongs" then we still arrive at the third branch representing King Charles III ascending the throne at 3:10 pm on the 8th of September, 2022.

So, let's examine the second part,

which is essentially all about the fulfilment of the dream *in its second degree!*

Let's break the forgoing statement about the second degree into its primary components:

1. "But at last,
2. this same Tree,
3. through the compassionate mercy of God,
4. and without any national (governmental) assistance,
5. shall return to its original root,
6. reflourish,
7. and bear abundant fruit."

Although much of this is obvious, I'll step through each point.

- "But at last,

This is a statement that says that 'everything which follows, 2 to 7, will *at last occur*'—they were always predestined!

437

- this same Tree,

This ensures that we realise that the green branches that started with George I are branches that are part of the **original** Tree—that is, they are branches reattached to the original Saxon root; the branches from George I **ARE NOT** figuratively growing on a separate tree!

- through the compassionate mercy of God,

This phrase is encouragement to those who have been faithful to God to be patient; it announces that God did indeed have a plan all along, and those who believe in the Four Great Prophecies of Arthurian Britain would be encouraged that in time, the Red Dragon will indeed rise to kill the White Dragon, and that in time, Arthur will return as a raven.

- and without any national (governmental) assistance,

438

This illustrates that the government cannot manipulate the fulfilment of this prophecy; its providence will be affected by the Hand of God—and by God alone.

- shall return to its original root,

This announces that the green branches already proven to be detached from the Tree by three furlongs will be reattached to the original Saxon root by the hand of God.

- reflourish,

This announces that The Branches of the Patrilineal Houses that are on the throne shall themselves reflourish into a luscious oaken canopy with equal significance as that canopy had prior to 1066.

- and bear abundant fruit."

This relates to the broad nature of the capacity of The Great Old British

Oak to bear abundant fruit, which in effect promises prosperity to every oaken family tree in Britain—implying that all of the indigenous natives of Britain will receive prosperity from the hand of God under the purview of the Great Old British Oak having been restored.

Having explained the detail of the symbols of the previous passage, I've traditionally grouped the last two together—in my mind, "(1) reflourish, and (2) bear abundant fruit" both fall under the topic of **flourishing**.

That is, a flourishing tree does indeed bear abundant fruit.

Naturally, we should not overlook the subtlety of the word "**re**flourish"—this means that the new *flourishing* will bear the same resemblance of the predestiny of the original Tree's flourishing.

The importance of this should be underlined—the reflourishing will not be the flourishing of new contexts but the reflourishing of those Celtic ideals that Arthur and his army of Britons were originally fighting to protect.

So, this brings us to the need to examine what this new 'flourishing' will look like:

1. What will the reflourishing look like? And,
2. What will the dropping of abundant fruit look like?

Naturally, the fulfilment of Edward the Confessor's Deathbed Dream will need to be in accord with the Four Great Prophecies of Arthurian Britain, and here lays a subtle answer to these questions.

We've discovered so far that the reason why William the Conqueror was used as an instrument of God to "cut down The Great Old British Oak" was because of England's great sins.

Clearly, those sins relate to the **marginalisation**, the **suppression**, and the **obfuscation** of the heritage of we ancient Britons—*our M-S-O—that which we seek to reclaim—that which will be 'reflourished'*.

Here, I hope that you will also realise that as an Orthodox Celt, I've referred to myself as an "Ancient Briton": we are the heirs of our indigenous ancestors, and as such, we in the present have become them of our past!

One of the problems of this modern age is that many people claim to be Britons who, at best, can be described as British. The usefulness of calling oneself an Ancient Briton in this modern age is that it not only attaches one's heritage to our ancestors, the ancient Britons of this land, but it also asserts that we, as Ancient Britons, are their Indigenous heirs—that is, as Ancient Britons, we

442

are "Britons of the line of Arthur", not "Britons falsely claimed who are at best British".

Therefore, the fulfilment of Edward the Confessor's Deathbed Dream **in its second degree** relates to the progressive reinstitution of the culture of we Ancient Britons in Britain—the restoration of our M-S-O—that is, the restoration of our heritage that has been marginalised, suppressed, and obfuscated!

Broadly, this will manifest as a Celtic Revival, and my hope is that it will spread to other parts of Europe with Celtic roots.

The News Flash is that all of us with at least nine generations of Celtic heritage should be allocated our fair share of land *by birthright,* upon which we should be able to live a self-sustainable lifestyle!

On an aside—and to reinforce this

prospect given the likelihood for modern bigots to try and troll this prospect—I'll merely mention that in recent decades, over 593 million acres of land have been returned to the Australian Aborigines under their claims of native title—we are no different in that we (Indigenous) Britons also have claims of Native Title.

Perhaps what is most straightforward to define—and which may still be quite far off from being achieved—is the guaranteed eventualities of the prophecies that "Arthur will return as a raven" and that "The Red Dragon will rise and kill the White Dragon", thus restoring indigenous Britain to its preordained future.

To fully explain this, one of the Four Great Prophecies of Arthurian Britain still needs to be fully resolved.

This will be addressed in my next book, "The Secret Cypher of Why There Are Ravens in The Tower of

London".

The solution is in the prophecy's qualifier, "**So long as...**":

- *"So long as* there are Ravens in The Tower of London, England will be protected."

1. On what basis are those 'ravens' in The Tower of London?
2. How are these 'ravens' in The Tower "as if 'chained' to The Tower of London"?
3. On what basis can these 'ravens' be **released from** The Tower of London?

Naturally, when the ravens are released from The Tower of London—just as when they were released from Noah's Ark—they will fly back and forth across the false spirits of the age, beating their wings to dry that flood water from all the earth: only then will the Dove of Peace be released!

Until you read that book, please be satisfied that when The Four Great Prophecies of Arthurian Britain are fulfilled, every indigenous Briton who has been in Britain for nine generations or more will be entitled to their fair share of land by birthright.

This is just one thing that Arthur and his army of Britons fought to protect!

And where it will take three generations for an immigrant to naturalise as an Indigenous Briton, those who have achieved their fourth generation but have not yet achieved their ninth will be entitled to a minimal croft by the simple birthright of being an Indigenous Briton, despite they not yet having achieved the ninth descent.

I dream of crusty apple pies made of produce that has been produced on my own self-sustainable farm, built on land that I've acquired by indigenous Celtic birthright!

Colophon

As a 'finishing touch' I'd like to dwell on the nature of "The Celtic Eagle"— that is, the 'eagle of evangelism' that carries the awen of what you have learned in this book!

I haven't written this book for it to be discussed in legalistic terms—instead, I've written it for its content to be carried 'on the wings of eagles'.

For example, let's say I'd expressed the analogy that the ancient Greek use of the word *Keltoi* to identify those Celts to whom this word was applied had the same general meaning as the ancient Kings of England using the Old English word for *Welsh* to identify Celts, but in another language and another context.

There's truth in saying that the word *Welsh* has the same general meaning as the word *Keltoi* but in the tongue of the English.

In that sense, the word **Welsh**—as carried on the wings of an eagle—can be seen to broadly mean 'Brythonic Celt'.

If you look at the parallels between these words, you should be able to see the truth that this analogy expresses!

And yet someone who was drawn along by the destructive Spirit of Legalism could quite easily attempt to provoke others by shifting their argument to something that is contrary to the original, faithful and truthful, intended meaning.

Yet no matter how someone might argue something contrary to the intended meaning, such as bringing up the actual fact that the etymologies of both words have different roots, the simple matter is that my original expression has meaning, is truthful, and has useful contexts where it can be usefully expressed. People who are driven by a destructive Spirit of Legalism can often be identified when their arguments against us are nothing more than a 'bait and switch'!

I encourage you to learn to identify the "legalistic bait" that they often lay in front to try and get you to "switch" to a destructive view.

Take heed, remember, you were borne on the wings of an eagle; you are not rats whose every intent is to drag an argument down any old hole into the depths of a sewer!

We are the proud heirs of our forefathers. We recognise that "Arthur will return as a raven". As Orthodox Celts, our message is designed to be borne on the wings of eagles. So *be* that eagle; search for the intended meaning!

To be baptised in the Word of God, all one needs to do is stand still and let the rising tide of The Truth around us take care of The Four Great Prophecies of Arthurian Britain fulfilling themselves!

If you have already read Annexes A and B, proceed to the Epilogue on Page 473.

Annexe A

Reproduced from my book
"The Secret Cypher of Chalice Well"

An Introduction to Cyphers!

Note: this refers to another book, see above!

Before starting our adventure to discover the meaning of the Secret Cypher of Chalice Well, we must first become good Code Breakers!

A Cypher is like a secret handshake where both people know about a shared secret and refuse to share information unless both parties know the secret.

Imagine shaking hands with someone who didn't know your Secret Handshake. Would you share your secret information with them? No, of course, you wouldn't!

Flesch—68; Reading time—6:11; Speaking time—11:53

The exciting thing about a Secret Handshake is that you don't have to know the other person to determine whether or not you should share a secret with them. All you have to know is a pre-arranged secret that authenticates them with you!

If the person you shake hands with proves to you that they already know the Secret Handshake, then you may consider them authenticated because the first secret you would have shared was the Secret Handshake itself!

Once a person is authenticated, you can share with them any secret you want to share with the confidence that they are authorised to receive it.

There are many types of secret codes, and Secret Handshakes are just one type of code. The purpose of a Secret Handshake has just one thing in mind: to authenticate that another person can be trusted with secrets.

Cyphers are all about trust. You need to be confident about the secrets that they are based upon.

Curiously, I have already shown you a new Cypher without you knowing it—and the reason you don't know it is because you don't yet have the Cypher's Secret Key.

I have spelt the word "Cypher" using the old spelling instead of the modern spelling of "Cipher".

The Secret Key here is the knowledge that those of us who continue to use the old spelling are in a special type of club where we like trying to discover ancient secrets. We call ourselves *Cyphers*.

On the following page, I'll show you an extract from a famous author from the nineteenth century where she used the old spelling.

The famous author who wrote this was Jane Austen, and this is from her book titled Mansfield Park. It was originally published in 1814.

Can you see how cleverly the word Cypher is being used here?

Lady Bertram seems more of a cypher now than when he is at home; and nobody else can keep Mrs. Norris in order.

"Lady Bertram seems more of a cypher now than when he is at home ; and nobody else can keep Mrs. Norris in order." ...

Jane Austen was writing that Lady Bertram appears to fade into the background or become less noticeable in Sir Thomas Bertram's absence. But what could this mean?

What is the secret implication?

• One possible meaning is that Lady Bertram becomes secretive when her husband is not around. That might imply that Lady Bertrum was having a secret affair behind Sir Thomas' back!

- Another possible reason is that Lady Bertrum lacks individuality or significance, often blending into the background or being overshadowed by others.

Which is it? Without knowing the Cypher Key, we don't have the answer to what the author was implying when she used the word Cypher!

In this case, the 'Cypher Key' is the knowledge that Jane Austen was writing about women who didn't have as much power or freedom as men did, and because of this, we can presume that Lady Bertrum was not having a secret affair, but instead that she tended to fade into the background when her husband was not around.

Cyphers come in different forms!

Some are messages that are secretly encoded into conversation, just like how Jane Austen conveyed otherwise concealed notions about Lady Bertrum. This form of Cypher is called "Double Entendre", where additional knowledge is the key that allows us to make plausible assumptions about a secret being expressed.

Secret agents might use double entendres as a form of covert communication or to convey hidden messages to fellow agents or contacts while maintaining plausible deniability in case of interception or surveillance.

As super-sleuths, we can pretend we are decoding intercepted messages:

• **Code Words**: Secret agents might use innocent-sounding words or phrases with double meanings to convey specific instructions or information. For example, "The eagle flies at midnight" could be a double entendre where "eagle" represents a specific target or objective, and "midnight" indicates a specific time or location for action.

- **Safe Phrases**: Double entendres could be used as safe phrases to confirm identities or signal readiness for a covert operation. Innocuous phrases like "The weather is lovely today" might have a hidden meaning understood only by agents involved in the operation.

- **Confirmation of Plans**: Agents might use double entendres to confirm plans or coordinate actions without explicitly stating details. For instance, "I'll pick up the package on my way home" could refer to an actual package or could be code for retrieving sensitive information.

- **Alerts or Warnings**: Double entendres could be used to alert fellow agents of danger or to convey warnings discreetly. A phrase like "The cat is in the garden" might signal that a location is compromised or that surveillance is in place.

- **Misdirection**: Double entendres could also be used to mislead adversaries or throw off suspicion. Agents might deliberately use ambiguous language or double meanings to confuse eavesdroppers or interceptors.
- **Cypher Overlays:** This technique involves placing a transparent or semi-transparent template over a known map or document, with the template containing encoded information such as letters, numbers, or symbols. When aligned correctly, the template reveals the answers or hidden message of the double entendre.

Other forms of Cypher are complicated, however we are going to begin our adventures in this book by taking a secret symbol and we will lay it over a map to see what secret location that the Cypher reveals.

Note: this refers to another book, as before!

The curious thing about the location

457

of this discovery is that we will need to decode its nature as well!

There's a Rule of Three when it comes to cracking ancient Cyphers:

- If you crack a Cypher that leads to a second Cypher, and you then crack the second Cypher, and in finding that it leads to a third Cypher, then cracking the third Cypher will most likely open up a new topic of research that has never been discovered.

The lesson here is that if you crack three Cyphers in an 'embedded chain of three', then you will most likely become that topic's leading expert!

Our journey is going to lead us into the exciting nature of the Arthurian realm, where there is plenty of information that will allow us to make many plausible assumptions that will most likely reveal even further Cyphers to resolve.

We will even resolve Cyphers three layers deep, so who knows, you may even spy some hidden Cyphers that still need to be cracked!

Sometimes, a good way to disguise a secret is in a poem, and when you research Arthurian topics, you will often find that ancient secrets were actually hidden in ancient Welsh poetry.

Secrets that are hidden in poems are often more loosely expressed, yet by now you should understand everything that I have written in the following composition.

Would you have understood this if I had not written this previous introduction to it?

Helpful Tip: You should practice writing your own poetry when you can because by learning to encode secrets into your own poetry, you will become better at cracking other people's Secret Cyphers!

The Secret Quest of Chalice Well

In the land of quests and hidden lore,
Where secrets wait behind each door,
We start our journey, bold and free,
To crack the code of mystery.

But 'ere we tread the path unknown,
We must first learn to break the tone
Of cyphers guarding secrets deep,
In hidden realms where legends sleep.

A cypher's like a secret dance,
A handshake shared, a whispered trance,
Where trust is built on whispered words,
And secrets shared, once they're assured.

Imagine shaking hands, you see,
With one who lacks the cypher key.
Would you unveil your secrets grand
To one who doesn't understand?

No! For in the world of code,
Trust is earned on secret roads.
The hand you shake must know the way,
To unlock what the cypher may say.

Jane Austen, in her tales so old,
Crafted cyphers, secret troves
With words she wove a secret thread,
A world of meaning left unsaid.

In Mansfield Park, the cypher gleams,
In Lady Bertram's whispered dreams.

The Secret Cypher of Edward The Confessor

She fades away when Thomas leaves,
What secrets lie beneath the eaves?

Perhaps a love, a hidden fire,
Or simply one who will retire
To shadows deep when light is gone,
Her presence fading like the dawn.

Cyphers come in many forms,
From whispered words to hidden norms.
But in our quest, we'll start with one,
A symbol laid beneath the sun.

We'll overlay it on a map,
To find the secrets it may trap.
And if we crack the chain of three,
The path to Camelot we'll see.

Through Arthur's realm, we'll boldly tread,
Where secrets sleep in realms widespread.
And as we journey, day by day,
New cyphers will unveil their way.

So join us on this winding road,
Where secrets wait to be bestowed.
For in the world of code breakers bold,
The greatest tales are yet not told.

Imagine if someone found this poem
in a thousand years, it doesn't even
mention the Secret Cypher of Chalice
Well. And yet it does, a super-sleuth
would find it then crack it!

461

Annexe B

Edited extracts from my book
"The Secret Cypher of Chalice Well"

Special Definitions

*A Fast Track Introduction to
Specialised Terms used by the
Science of Secret Cyphers*

Decombobulating the Science of Secret Cyphers

As you can imagine, we Secret Cypher Super Sleuths use specialised terms related to the Science of Secret Cyphers.

Cyphers tend to be composed of intricately connected elements that have already been disguised, so when we are presented with a new Secret Cypher, we first want to "decombobulate" it.

Flesch—50; Reading time—4:51; Speaking time—9:19

The word **decombobulate** means to disassemble something into its essential components, and as you can imagine, to **combobulate** something means to put its essential components together.

And, of course, if something previously a **combobulation** had been **decombobulated**, and you then combobulate it again—you can say that it was **recombobulated**, becoming a **recombobulation**.

However, I generally don't use the word recombobulate because knowing it was previously a combobulation rarely adds value to a quest!

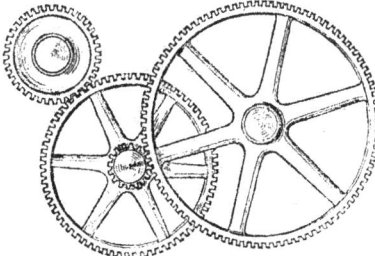

A Secret Cypher is like a series of ideas that have been put together yet you have to work out what the cogs are and how they are arranged!

Secret Cypher Vocabulary

You should add the following words to your Secret Cypher vocabulary.

1. **Combobulate.** To put essential components together.
2. **Decombobulate.** To disassemble something into its essential components.
3. **Combobulation.** The assembly of those things that have been combobulated.
4. **Discombobulate.** To confuse a series of essential components so that they or their combobulation are not easily seen.
5. **Discombobulation.** A sphere where a combobulation is thought to exist, which, if being so, has been successfully obfuscated.

The last two relate to how we cleverly create Secret Cyphers ourselves.

The whole point of a Cypher is to be secret when needed but capable of

464

being decyphered when necessary.

Naturally, a Secret Cypher Super Sleuth must also master the skill of obfuscating (or confusing) a Cypher's essential components.

This is especially important when we Cyphers want to be able to create Secret Cyphers as well as to crack them!

Examples that use these words

I've prepared a series of examples that illustrate these terms. However, I'll first need to explain the context of how these words are typically used!

As a fast-track introduction to these words, I've written these specific examples to illustrate how **machinery** is composed—the two allegories I use are excellent!

Although this may surprise you, it is helpful to imagine that a Cypher is a clockwork mechanism where each idea is as though it is a "cog" in a clockwork gear-train mechanism.

In such a gear train, one "cog" of an idea directly engages with another "cog" of an idea—and the net result is that the Secret Cypher is 'the time that is told' by the mechanism as a whole!

The "cogs" themselves are the clues, and your job as a Cypher is to identify those cogs and then assemble them into a clockwork mechanism that "correctly tells the time".

Although you will typically start your quest with the realisation that the different parts "of the clockwork mechanism" are your clues, you should also realise that you will typically start with all of these ideas as though they were a collection of random cogs that "have been dumped into the 'bucket' of your mind".

So your job is:

1. To identify each of these cogs;
2. To sort each of these cogs by determining how they all relate to each other;
3. To arrange them so that from one cog bearing upon another cog, that they all tend to turn in complete harmony with each other;
4. To cause a specific predestined arrangement of the cogs to cause the correct 'time' to be told.

The clever thing about comparing a Secret Cypher to a clockwork mechanism that tells the time is that you can also imagine that each tooth of any particular cog is a **synonym** of the idea **central** to that specific cog!

All of the synonyms surrounding the cog relate to the central idea of that particular cog itself!

As such, you should be able to imagine that a Secret Cypher is a series of ideas surrounded by synonyms, which are the teeth that engage with the synonym teeth of the other cogs!

With that in mind, let's look at the following examples of how each word might be used:

1. **Combobulate:** After hours of meticulous work, the engineers managed to combobulate the intricate machinery, aligning each gear and circuit into perfect harmony.
2. **Decombobulate:** With a swift twist of the screwdriver, the technician began to decombobulate the device, dismantling it into its parts for inspection.
3. **Combobulation:** The completion of the project marked the successful combobulation of all the scattered ideas and resources into a coherent and functional system.
4. **Discombobulate:** The unexpected influx of data seemed to discombobulate the system, causing errors and confusion among its es-

sential components.

5. **Discombobulation:** In the midst of the investigation, the detectives found themselves in a state of discombobulation, surrounded by clues that seemed to lead nowhere, obscuring the underlying combobulation of the case.

Although I've used a mechanical allegory to show how a train of ideas can bear down upon each other as though they were a series of cogs that collectively tell the time, it should not be too difficult for you to realise that Language Cyphers are just like cogs in a clock that tells the time!

In that sense, different ideas are the cogs, but the time that the cogs cause to be displayed is the answer to the Secret Cypher.

Another useful illustration is that of a weaving mill, where the 'looming of ideas' is represented by coloured threads wound around a series of weaving bobbins, which are woven by the loom into the final tapestry, where the Secret Cypher is the picture that the tapestry portrays.

- In this sense, the Science of Secret Cyphers is all about identifying and sorting 'bobbins' in our mind;
- It's where the coloured thread of one bob interweaves with the coloured thread of another bob that all the threads are cleverly woven together, as though each bobbin thread were a Secret Key that could be rediscovered.

Naturally, these 'bobbins' are the 'bobs' being manipulated by each process—such as com**bob**ulation, decom**bob**ulation, etcetera!

As a finishing touch, I'll also say that the phrase "… and Bob's your uncle!" becomes very useful in the Super Sleuth community, and that is because how the word 'bob' (from bobbin) implies that there is a 'thread' that connects between one idea and another—or between a series of ideas.

The essence of this is that when someone says, "And Bob's your uncle!" they are indicating that the solution to a particular quest has been found!

A popular theory suggests that this phrase originated in the United Kingdom in the late 19th century, during the time of British Prime Minister Robert "Bob" Cecil.

It's believed that Cecil appointed his nephew, Arthur Balfour, to a high government position, leading to the phrase "Bob's your uncle", which implies that success or a favourable outcome was assured through obvious connections.

Of course, Secret Keys are created when we intentionally confuse these 'bobbins', and the same politics of the time tried to obfuscate the relationship of the Prime Minister's nephew to him to avoid the connection itself being seen as contributory.

This is where the subject of 'veiled speech' becomes a useful political tool!

Veiled Speech is the expression of Secret Cyphers that are 'as if under a veil', or 'obfuscated'.

I hope that this annexe has been a useful introduction to these words and insightful for when you come across them in this book!

If you read this annexe because you were directed to do so in Chapter One, you should now proceed to Chapter Two.

Epilogue

The aroma of freshly baked crusty Apple Pie has been savoured in Britain since time immemorial, taking us back to at least the Druids of Caesar's time.

Indeed, pie pastry as we know it has been in Europe since as early as the 5th century BC—and this was a long time before the United States of America 'nationalised' the Apple Pie, sometime after the early pilgrims arrived at Plymouth Rock in 1620.

Yet Arthurian history is just as much part of America's heritage as the Apple Pie is, and this is because wherever we Celts have travelled from Britain, our Arthurian heritage has travelled with us.

This prospect opens up the Arthurian Tale to the whole world, and I imagine that our stories are just as familiar to anyone worldwide as is the wonderful aroma of a freshly baked Apple Pie.

The curious thing about this is that the more that we Britons rediscover the Secret Cyphers of our own Arthurian heritage, then the more likely it will be of interest to others worldwide, wherever the original stories have spread.

In my last book, *The Secret Cypher of Chalice Well,* I introduced readers to hundreds of Celtic Secret Cyphers.

I expanded on these in this book, *The Secret Cypher of Edward the Confessor,* and common to both of these books is the ancient understanding that those who had lived in a Celtic kingdom for nine generations or more had the **birthright** to be allocated free plots of land so that they could live a fully self-sustainable lifestyle.

474

In Britain, these plots of land are supposed to have been at least five acres in size, and that's because in this part of the world, five acres is about the smallest area of land that a small family needs for self-sustainability.

The essence here, is that the Fulfilment of Edward the Confessor's Deathbed Dream implies that one day in the future—far or near—everyone who has lived in Britain for nine generations or more will be entitled to such free land: no longer will they be mortgaged by a dead-pledge to suffer 20 years of paying off a small home, they will instead be given a small farm-sized plot of land when they come of age and are married.

The concept of a citizen of a country receiving their fair share of land **by birthright** is not new—it was actually the ordinary practice in Britain before the Anglo-Saxons turned this wonderful isle's system of governance on its head.

Just as the aroma of a freshly baked Apple Pie lifts the soul, I hope that every time that someone catches the sweet aroma of this blessed bundle of joy, that they also take time to think that maybe it's fair and proper to start thinking that people, worldwide, should receive a small parcel of land for free, **by birthright**, just because their family has existed on the land for at least nine generations.

This is the Arthurian dream, and according to the Four Great Prophecies of Arthurian Britain, the history of Britain is predestined to revert to its natives being able to enjoy these benefits.

Naturally, the question is "When will this happen?", and this is a question which I'll explore in my next book, "The Secret Cypher of Why There are Ravens in The Tower of London".

Naturally, most people worldwide with a British connection have heard the prophecy "So long as there are ravens in The Tower of London, England will be protected!", and this gives us a little clue.

The concept of 'England being protected' alludes to the preservation of Anglo-Saxon culture in Britain, but the expression of "So long as ..." alludes to the matter that sometime in the future, the ravens will be released from The Tower of London so that the culture of we native Britons can be restored.

My hope is that by the time that you read that next book, that when you serve Apple Pie as the dessert that follows your main dinner course at home, that you'll raise the following toast:

"Let's drink to the day when we natives will be given free land by birthright—enough to plant an orchard of apple trees of our own so that we can become what we sow!"

- (Refrain:) **"To Apple Pies!"**

It's not for us to dismiss the prospect of this happening, and that's because we Orthodox Celts believe in the prophecy "Arthur will return as a raven!"

This means that by the time that Arthur does return, the politicians of his age will have worked out a pathway so that exercising this birthright will not just be possible, but will be equitable.

To Apple Pies!

About the Author

Anthony Harrison

'Harrison of The North of Branthwaite'

May Day Celebrations at Penrith—No amount of rain will wash Anthony away!

Family Background

The author—by Coat of Arms, *Harrison of The North of Branthwaite*—belongs to a distinctive indigenous class in the County of Cumberland,

479

Great Britain, known as "Statesmen".

This group constitutes numerous native inhabitants of Cumberland who are recognised as Statesmen, where the patriarchal heads of these families are called a Statesman.

By large, these Statesmen settled in Cumberland post-945 AD when it was part of Scotland, who underwent a process of naturalisation over three generations, evolving into Britons. Their patriarch eventually attained the status of Clan Chief. However, following Cumberland's return to England under the Treaty of York in 1237 AD and the subsequent decline of Norman French as the primary language of governance in England, they came to be known as Statesmen in English.

This naming evolution traces back to the original Old Welsh that was spoken in Cumberland, where the term "pencenedl" denoted a leader or chief, translating to "head of the kindred" or "chief of the people/clan". During Scottish rule over Cumberland, this term translated into the king's tongue as "Ard-Cheannard" or "Ceannard na Clann" in Scots Gaelic, signifying "leader of the clan". This naming transition then continued through Norman French, which the new English Kings adopted after the Norman Conquest, signifying "chief of the clan" or "chief of the family", culminating in the adoption of the English term "Statesman" by around the 14th century.

In Cumberland, the rank of Statesman equates to that of a Clan Chief in Scotland, and these terms are now interchangeable in English. This equivalence aligns with the concept that a Clan Chief originally presided over their own client-state in Scotland between 945 and 1237 AD.

During this period, the King of Scots recognised no difference between the Chiefs of Cumberland and the Chiefs of Strathclyde. His acknowledgement of them as leaders of their respective client-states reflected his system of power brokering that accommodated the wave of an influx of numerous new leaders and their retinues from distant lands into Cumberland and Strathclyde—becoming an intrinsic part of the Celtic system during that era.

The origin story of The Harrisons of The North is quite interesting, who arrived in Cumberland in 1056 AD, hailing from the region around Tongeren, the oldest city in modern-day Belgium, who rose from the remnants of the Celtic Tungri tribe, springing forth from their ancestor, the Duke of Habspruch, who although formerly a Celtic bishop, became an ecclesiastic prince when acquiring the responsibilities of a departing Roman Commander as a hereditary role, when the western Roman Empire was collapsing.

Because of this heritage, these 'Harusons', whose branch of the Habspruchs meant Golden Strength, acquired the territorial epithet 'of The North' when Royal Heralds needed it to distinguish them from other 'Harrison' sounding names who were merely 'sons of Harry'. As such, the name Harrison of The North is connected to their Coat of Arms.

The Author

Anthony, the present head of this ancient family, has followed in his father's footsteps as an indigenous land rights activist, who, just like his father, who served in 22 SAS, the Blues and Royals of the Household Cavalry, and MI5, also has Special Forces experience. He has served as a Commissioned Officer in the Regular Army, served proudly with the Honourable Artillery Company in London, and developed quite a reputation for supporting indigenous land rights when running the Cumbric Revival Community Forum in the noughties, whom BBC Radio Cumbria occasionally interviewed.

Anthony appeared on First Dates in 2017, and, in his own words, he 'still needs an heir and a spare'.

If Anthony is to be compared with someone, it should probably be Eddie Mabo, an Australian Aborigine with little education and a rural upbringing, who started an indigenous land rights movement that resulted in over 593 million acres being returned to the Australian Aborigines.

Anthony is cut from the same cloth, who, as a First Nation Aboriginal of Cumberland, is seeking similar restitution for every native of Cumberland who has been in Cumberland for more than three generations, but in their own uniquely indigenous context.

He is fearless, stands the ground of

his fellow Marra without question, and is one of few specialists with such vibrant perspective and depth of knowledge about Cumberland's indigenous affairs: it was Anthony who discovered that the "Secret Symbol of The Red Dragon" at Glastonbury identifies the exact location of King Arthur's Round Table!

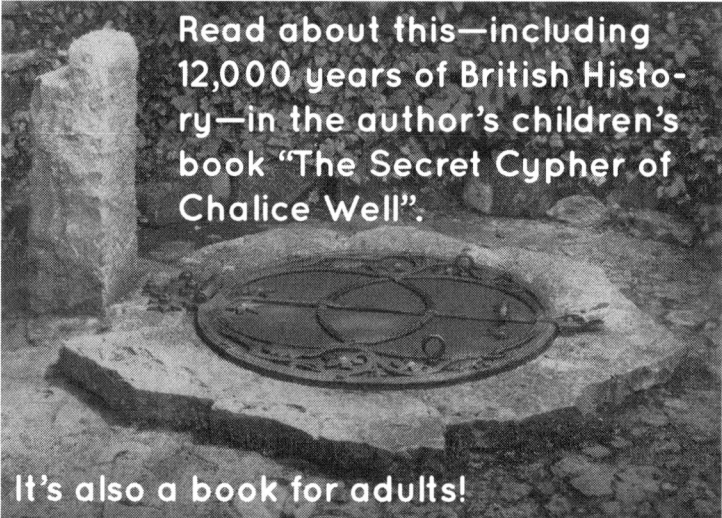

Read about this—including 12,000 years of British History—in the author's children's book "The Secret Cypher of Chalice Well".

It's also a book for adults!

Centre of mainland Great Britain
Location of the henge called King Arthur's Round Table, known in Old Welsh as "Penrith", which means "Chief meeting place of the leaders of Britain".

Glastonbury

©

485

Merchandise
www.habspruch.com

See website for full colour!

Merchandise bearing the painting "The Crux of Arthurian Canon" by Ben Waddams.

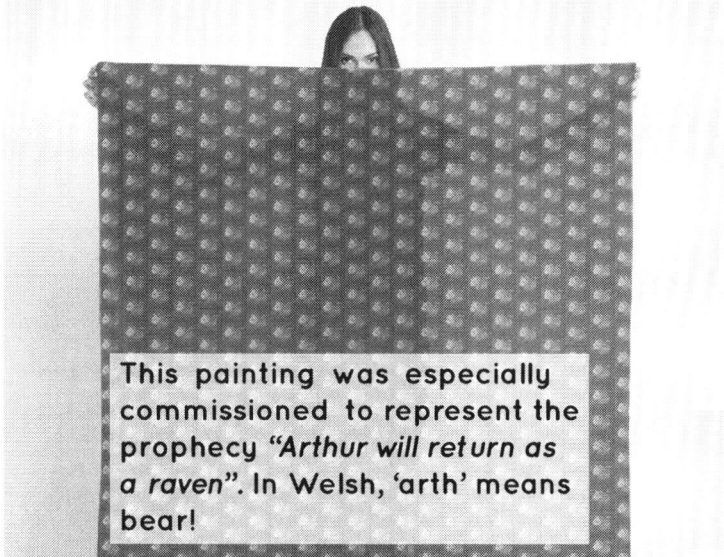

This painting was especially commissioned to represent the prophecy *"Arthur will return as a raven"*. In Welsh, 'arth' means bear!

The Secret Cypher of Edward The Confessor

99+
Products

See website
for full colour!

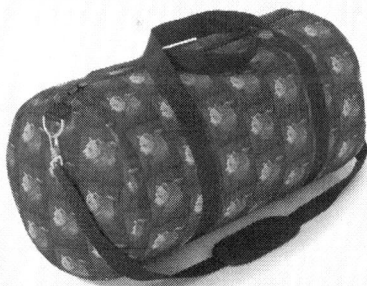

Merchandise

www.habspruch.com
See website for full colour!

487

Harrison of The North of Branthwaite

99+
Products

See website
for full colour!

Merchandise
www.habspruch.com
See website for full colour!

.

Printed in Great Britain
by Amazon

283d6f39-48e1-45e0-8223-6493cb72a46eR01